Beth

Small
Miracles
from Beyond

꩜

Also available by Yitta Halberstam and Judith Leventhal

Small Miracles for Women:
Extraordinary Coincidences of Heart and Spirit

Small Miracles from Beyond

DREAMS, VISIONS and SIGNS that LINK US to the OTHER SIDE

YITTA HALBERSTAM &
JUDITH LEVENTHAL

STERLING ETHOS
New York

STERLING ETHOS
New York

An Imprint of Sterling Publishing
387 Park Avenue South
New York, NY 10016

ISBN 978-1-4549-1284-2

Distributed in Canada by Sterling Publishing
^c/o Canadian Manda Group, 165 Dufferin Street
Toronto, Ontario, Canada M6K 3H6
Distributed in the United Kingdom by GMC Distribution Services
Castle Place, 166 High Street, Lewes, East Sussex, England BN7 1XU
Distributed in Australia by Capricorn Link (Australia) Pty. Ltd.
P.O. Box 704, Windsor, NSW 2756, Australia

For information about custom editions, special sales, and premium and
corporate purchases, please contact Sterling Special Sales at 800-805-5489
or specialsales@sterlingpublishing.com.

Manufactured in the United States of America

2 4 6 8 10 9 7 5 3 1

www.sterlingpublishing.com

For my husband, Motty, whose goodness and kindness is beyond this world.

~ *Yitta Halberstam*

To my father, Hershel Frankel, and my uncle and aunt, Isser and Malku Handler. From the ashes of the Holocaust, you built lives that were purposeful and inspirational. *That* is Beyond.

~ *Judith Leventhal*

Contents

🙙🙘

PREFACE

*D*eep in the hearts of most people a great fear of ran-domness resides. We wrestle with the disquieting sense that the events in our lives are haphazard and meaning-less, and that the challenges of human existence may simply have no point. During dark nights of the soul, when we are visited—and wracked—by the big questions we successfully avoid during our frenzied activity during sunlit hours, we ask: Why am I here? Where did I come from? What's my role in the big picture? Why is there a universe? Are we alone in the cosmos? Is there a divine intelligence behind the appearance of space, time, energy, matter, gravity?

Beyond theology's mission to fill the void and unravel the complexities of life, simple human stories also bring reassurance to those who seek the validation that human existence does matter, that everything (and everyone) is part of a Greater Plan.

When *Small Miracles: Extraordinary Coincidences from Everyday Life* (the first book in the seven-volume series) origi-nally debuted in 1997, it struck a nerve with the American public and was embraced with enthusiasm by those who yearned to find pattern and purpose in their personal worlds. By offering a spiritual perspective on coincidences, and affirming the thesis that human beings are connected to one another (indeed, to all the variegated forms of life) in a unified way, *Small Miracles* struck down the concepts of luck, fate, and chance as mere illusions—concepts that stood in the way of greater enlighten-ment and spiritual elevation. By recounting the true stories of amazing coincidences that occurred in ordinary people's lives, *Small Miracles* provided readers with comforting confirmation that the events in their lives were consequential, and that even more so, they themselves were sacred human beings whose lives were laden with intention and significance. Two weeks after its publication, *Small Miracles* jumped onto all the major best-seller lists and sold close to one million copies in the United States alone (it was translated into sixteen foreign languages as well), testifying to the enduring hunger of readers for outward signs that we count, and that we interact with whatever is "out there" in a dynamic way.

But there are still other questions over which we agonize: those revolving not around life itself, but death, its punctuation mark. How does it all end? What happens when my heart stops beating, my lungs stop ventilating, my liver stops detoxifying? Do I just disappear? Everything that I did on this earth during my lifetime—all my skills, my knowledge, my memories, the things that make me *me*—do they just get sucked up into a gargantuan black hole, or do they get transported somewhere else? I know that my physical body will decompose, but what happens to its animating force—my soul? Is it immortal . . . does it somehow go on? And if it does, where exactly does it go to? What about my loved ones? What happens to my relationships with them? All the soul connections that were the nectar of my life . . . all the love that was shared during our short time on earth—do these things too inexorably vanish with death?

The stories in the first seven books of the Small Miracles series focused primarily on the questions readers ask about life. In a departure from our past mandate, this new book takes a leap into the great beyond and mirrors the ongoing fascination of American readers with the more numinous aspects of the human journey by focusing on stories related to the experience of "death."

Despite—or perhaps because of—its topic, *Small Miracles from Beyond* is an uplifting book providing solace and succor for those who have lost significant others or who are facing serious illness themselves. The stories on these pages illustrate premises posited by some of today's most popular books: namely, that life never ends; that there is a different plane or dimension into which we enter after the cessation of life as we know it; that consciousness does not cease to exist merely because the physical body to which it is attached has expired; and that when a loved one dies, the soul-connection that he or she has forged with friends and relatives is not obliterated but remains eternal. This everlasting bond is expressed by the continuous involvement of the deceased in the lives of those the person leaves behind. Parents continue to watch over the lives of their children, deriving pride in their accomplishments and interceding on their behalf before the heavenly throne. Indeed, the Zohar (the most fundamental work of Kabbalah) tells us that if it were not for the intercession of our loved ones residing above, our world below could not endure for even a moment. Deceased relatives are kept extremely busy by the activities of the living in other ways as well, the Zohar goes on to say. Their souls "come down" to participate in the joyous occasions of their descendants (births and weddings, for example)—a belief that is the basis for an old Jewish tradition of visiting the cemetery before a wedding to invite the souls of family members to attend.

The first law of thermodynamics states that no energy is ever lost or destroyed; it only assumes another form. If *physical* energy never dissipates and instead is recycled, what shall we assume about spiritual energy, the energy of the soul—whose existence is not limited by time, space, or any of the other delineators of the physical state?

Since the beginning of civilization, a belief in some form of life after death has dominated practically every society. In many cultures, people believed that the supernatural world often communicated with the natural world through dreams, in which dreamers received words of wisdom and counsel. There are numerous accounts in the Bible of dreams of great import, and records report that as early as 145 CE the famed Greek physician Galen turned to the study of medicine as a result of a dream his father had.

Today, the shelves of bookstores brim over with myriad memoirs of near-death experiences, communication with the deceased, and other mystical/supernatural experiences. This book provides a unique format for telling these tales: *Small Miracles from Beyond* contains a series of short stories from ordinary people from all over the world who testify with their dramatic, mysterious, and compelling tales that we are not alone in the universe, and that not only is God carrying us, but our deceased relatives and loved ones are supporting us as well. Their presence continues to bless us in the small, personal, and ordinary events we experience every day, events that may very well provide important clues or small hints that they are with us still. Sadly, some of us are not attuned to the messages of the coincidences, even when we encounter them repeatedly. It is our fervent hope that this book will help open readers' eyes to the miracles that surround them, and consequently imbue them with a newfound appreciation for the awe, harmony, and unity that exist in the universe, and in life itself.

And for those who have undergone a painful loss and are in mourning, we pray that our book provides you with this comfort and knowledge: Your loved ones are with you still, and they shower blessings upon you every day.

Small Miracles
from Beyond

A CALL FROM HEAVEN

My mother was a "believer." Long before "New Age" had become a coined term and part of the national vernacular, my mother was already inhaling a host of psychological, self-improvement, spiritual, and mystical works by thinkers ranging from Alice Miller, Norman Vincent Peale, and Dale Carnegie to Edgar Cayce and Jeane Dixon. The outcome of all this reading was her firm conviction that the power of the personal will could transcend all situations (with the help of God, of course!) and her steadfast belief that another world existed beyond this earthly plane.

Consequently, when she died eight years ago at the young age of seventy-two, I was sure that if anyone could conceivably wend his or her way back to this world and deposit a sign in their children's laps that all was well in a different dimension, it would be my mother. I was, alas, sorely disappointed. I kept checking in with both my brother and sister, asking frequently: "Have you heard from Mommy yet?" OK, it was really a standing joke, but as the cliché goes, in every little joke resides a morsel of truth. After collecting hundreds of stories about ADC (after death communication) from readers of previous Small Miracles books, I decided it was time for one of my own. My mother, however, was not forthcoming.

Several years passed. I continued to mourn her deeply, and over time the void didn't lessen as much as I had expected it would. (I believe that the death of the second parent, no matter what the relationship, ends up being the more deadly blow because it renders the child—no matter what age—an irrevocable orphan.) Every day I thought of her, at least once.

One day I spoke out loud, addressing my mother in a jocular way: "Come on, Ma, where's the sign? For heaven's sake (no pun intended), you of all people should've sent me one by now!" But no bolt of lightning or fireworks display suddenly flared. Edgar Cayce would have been crestfallen to learn what a fiasco his body of work had ultimately been, how his posthumous tutelage had woefully failed to exert its influence on his most ardent disciple—my mother.

But a few hours later, close to midnight, the telephone suddenly rang. When I answered it, all I heard was a strange static that crackled over the wires. "Hello? Hello!" I kept shouting into the receiver. Who would call me so late at night if it wasn't an emergency . . . or a wrong number? Or was it a call from abroad that had somehow malfunctioned? Finally, exasperated, I hung up the phone and looked at the caller ID to determine the identity of the person who had tried to connect. I squinted at the numbers. That was strange! They read "000-000-000." Goose bumps ran up and down my spine.

Just then my husband strode through the front door (a Good Samaritan, he often keeps odd hours helping people in distress). "Did you just try to call me?" I demanded.

"No," he drew back defensively, fearing a spousal attack. "Didn't I call you just two hours ago? Why would I need to call you right before I came home?"

"Well, that's odd," I said, half spooked, half thrilled at the prospect I was already beginning to entertain in my mind. "Someone just called, didn't say a word, there was a lot of weird static on the line, and when I looked at the caller ID, it read: '000-000-000.'"

"Probably a telemarketer who doesn't want you to trace the call," my husband mumbled, as he poked his head into the refrigerator to scavenge.

"A telemarketer!" I screeched at his back. "No telemarketer calls at this hour!"

"So it was a wrong number," he replied. "Why are you making such a big deal about it?"

Then he whirled around to stare at me, his eyes rolling. "Aha!" he pounced. "You think it's from your mother, don't you? Which service do you think they use in Heaven? AT&T, Verizon, Sprint, Vonage?"

"Very funny," I said. "I know it sounds crazy, but I never received a call before whose caller ID read '000-000-000.' Have you?"

"No, but I'm sure there's a logical explanation for it."

"But the static was *strange*. And why would someone call so late at night if it wasn't an emergency, and if it was an emergency, wouldn't they call back a second time?"

"Because it was a wrong number, that's why! You are such a drama queen!" my husband yelled.

He ultimately convinced me that I was out of mind to even assume that a spectral spirit could make a long-distance call to Earth, and grudgingly I finally agreed. "Well, you can't say it isn't exciting to live with me!" I tried to joke. "Isn't it more fun to draw fanciful conclusions than more prosaic ones?" I asked.

I put the incident out of my mind, but I admit I was definitely let down that my mother hadn't made her presence known all these years.

I had practically forgotten the story until I started work on this book. I placed a call for true accounts on the Internet, besieged friends and family, scoured newspaper archives, magazines, and talk show and news show transcripts, and extensively researched various websites that post readers' stories. And on one such website, I found a narrative that was eerily similar to mine. In fact, it *could* have been mine. It was exactly the same.

"I asked my deceased mother for a sign that she was well in the dimension in which she dwelled," the contributor to the website wrote. "A few days later, the phone rang. When I picked it up, all I heard was static. When I examined the caller ID, the numbers that showed up were strange: '000-000-000.' I am convinced that the call came from my mother, because what kind of caller ID is that?"

I erupted into goose bumps once again as I read the woman's account—so strikingly familiar, an exact echo of my own experience. I began to wonder if any of my friends had ever received a phone call with that kind of caller ID. But everyone I canvassed said no.

Was my husband wrong? Had I in fact received a supernatural phone call coming from nowhere, as the numbers suggested? Or was there some logical reason behind the mystery, a veil that could be lifted to elucidate the cipher while simultane-ously eradicating the hope that leapt in my heart?

I guess I could have called the telephone company and been passed around from one customer service rep to another, as I tenaciously attempted to play sleuth and discover exactly what the strange caller ID meant. I wouldn't have been happy, though, if they had come up with an explanation that made sense. So I did exactly what any self-respecting daughter of a mother who read Edgar Cayce would do: absolutely nothing. I sat back and relished the experience. My mother had made that call, I con-vinced myself, and even if we hadn't had such great communica-tion while she was alive, now it was absolutely perfect.

~ *Yitta Halberstam*

THE CROSSWORD PUZZLE

*M*any people have recounted how their loved ones who passed over left a variety of signs to tell them that they were OK—including, among other things, flowers, feathers, butterflies, birds, and rainbows—but have you ever heard of the dead reaching out through a crossword puzzle? Yet that is precisely what happened to Joan Otto of East Lansing, Michigan, and her story was convincing enough to inspire jaded newspaper types to report her strange experience in the *East Lansing State Journal*. In fact, the account was so eerie and unusual that the writer of the story, who had worked for more than thirty years in the newspaper field, supposedly declared it the most unbelievable story he had ever reported.

In 1996, Joan's daughter Ruthie, twenty-seven, contracted—and survived—cervical cancer. A decade later, Ruthie and her husband decided to adopt a Lebanese baby boy, a brother to the daughter she had given birth to before the cancer. At the time of her trip to Lebanon to bring the baby home, she had felt instinctively that something was going awry in her body—she experienced unsettling symptoms that just didn't go away—but she was too intent on her mission to bring her new son home to pay attention. The Israel–Hezbollah war broke out during her visit. She would not leave without her son, whose paperwork was not finalized, and was thus marooned for several weeks during the height of the bombing.

Finally, she and her baby escaped with help from the American embassy; they were rescued by a naval ship in a rather cloak-and-dagger flight (she later appeared on the *Larry King* show to tell the story of her liberation).

Tragically, in the summer of 2008, the cancer returned and mercilessly took root in her body, invading other organs. Ruthie fought the good fight for several years, but by the time she was forty it had spread all over, and time was running out.

Ruthie's seventy-nine-year-old mother, Joan (a former newspaper reporter herself and still very active, despite her age), was a crossword-puzzle fiend who incessantly did the puzzles that appeared in the *East Lansing State Journal* each day. One day, as Ruthie, now forty, lay dying at home, her mother made an unusual request: "Ruthie, I know you're a good, church-going Catholic, quiet, reserved, and rational, not at all like me—into stuff you consider out of the box—but could you please do your old mother a favor? Could you let me know that you're OK? I don't need to know that you've met God, or that there are angels singing in Heaven, or any of that stuff. It's not that I need proof of the celestial realms. All I desperately need from you is a message that *you* are OK, that you are somewhere safe and happy in the great beyond. And to be sure that I know that the message is from you and from you only, can you please send it to me through a crossword puzzle?"

Laughing (despite her pain) at the mother whom everyone considered a "pistol," Ruthie agreed. She died on December 23, 2009, leaving behind her husband, two children, and many loved ones.

Over the next few months, Joan scoured the crossword puzzle daily, searching for some sign. She was sure that one would eventually come. But when it did, even she ended up being completely freaked out!

On June 21, 2010, Joan was in the bathroom working on the crossword puzzle, and as she filled in the blanks, her mind began to reel. No fewer than ten answers to that day's questions were inexorably linked to her daughter, Ruthie. It couldn't be a coincidence that there were ten—count 'em, ten—references that were very specific to her deceased daughter, could it? The blanks she filled in included the following clues:

1. The name RUTH (her daughter's name), which just happened to intersect with . . .

2. The name OTTO (her last name) . . .

3. Connecting to the word OK.

4. The answer BABE (Ruth's nickname; she was the baby in the family of four siblings, a midlife gift to her parents who came ten years after the birth of their youngest child), which bumps up against . . .

5. Another answer OK, appearing for a second time in the puzzle (crossword puzzles usually don't repeat answers).

6. The name RURU (another nickname the family used for Ruthie).

7. The name ERNIE down the middle of the puzzle (Ruth's middle name was Ernestine, and the family called her Ernie for short).

8. The letters EMT (Ruthie was employed as a neonatal intensive care nurse, and was qualified to care for newborns like an emergency medical technician).

9. The word WEE (Ruthie was qualified to put IVs into tiny babies, whom she often referred to as "the wee ones").

10. The word AMOK appeared as well; *amok* is usually defined as meaning "a frenzy," but when you're looking for signs, it could also conceivably be split into two words: "am OK."

Joan Otto's mouth went dry as she stared at the solved crossword puzzle. "I couldn't believe what I was reading," she says, vividly recalling the sequence of events of that fateful day. *"This just can't be happening! I thought. This can't be a coincidence. This is concrete. This is right in front of me."*

Although the newspaper was local, the crossword puzzles came from a national syndication service where no one knew or had even heard of the Ottos of East Lansing, Michigan. If the puzzles had been created locally, Joan could have reasoned that some kind acquaintance was trying to bring her solace or that a mean prank had been played. But the fact that the puzzles came from a far-away syndicate made the experience even more meaningful.

Trembling, Joan called Ruthie's husband and told him what she had discovered. A skeptic, he couldn't share Joan's enthusiasm or conviction . . . well, at least, at first. According to Joan, "He thought I was being pretty nutty, but when I went over to his home and showed him that day's newspaper, he was shocked. He just couldn't wrap his head around all the answers he read in that day's crossword puzzle."

Joan knows that many people probably laugh at her certainty that her daughter came to her in a crossword puzzle—believing that it was all just a "great big bundle of coincidences"—but her passionate belief that she did indeed receive a message from beyond this world remains unshaken.

"It wasn't only the tremendous comfort that I derived from the crossword puzzle that made me contact the newspaper," Joan says. "For me personally, I had received the assurance that my daughter was OK, and that was all I had asked for. She sent me the sign that I needed, and that was enough. The reason I went to the newspaper to publicize the story wasn't for me— it was for the world. I wanted everyone to know that there is more to life than just the earthly plane—there *is* something out there—something greater. People should know; it'll give them comfort and hope."

Joan says that since I first contacted her about the story, she's encountered two more crossword puzzle messages in the space of a month with special significance for her. "I had had no more crossword puzzle messages since the one I received from Ruthie in 2010. But since you contacted me about the story, all of a sudden I'm getting more messages."

"What could that possibly mean?" I asked Joan.

"You're supposed to write the story!"

Which I am dutifully doing. Right now.

~ Joan Otto, as told to the authors

A PAIR OF CARDINALS

A few years before my father, Francis Lenhart, died in February 2007 at the age of eighty-four, I bought him a book that I had read and loved—Fannie Flagg's *A Redbird Christmas*. I was an avid bird-watcher and had originally borrowed the book from the library—assuming it was about my favorite avocation—but it turned out to be a work of fiction, the bittersweet story of an abandoned little girl with a crippled leg and an older gentleman who befriends her. This man, named Oswald Campbell, has moved to a small town in Alabama with one grocery store and a "resident cardinal" to live out his last days (according to his doctor's prognosis). Oswald soon comes to play a very instrumental role in the young girl's life—helping her in many different ways and giving her, above all, the respect, love, attention, and faith she sorely lacks. When Oswald eventually dies, he returns to this earth as a cardinal in order to comfort the bereaved little girl.

I found *A Redbird Christmas* to be a very sweet and sentimental story, one that I just instinctively knew my father—a sucker for tenderness—would love. But it was off to the bookstore, not the library, for *his* copy. Christmas was coming, and what more appropriate gift than this one could I present?

My father, a hard-working banker, usually didn't have much time for reading. But he reported back to me that he had devoured the book in two days! Over the phone (we lived in different states), he told me that he had absolutely loved it! And then he said in a calm and resolute voice, "When I die, I'm also going to come back as a cardinal to comfort *you*!"

I shuddered at his casual reference to death. Even though he was getting on in years, I didn't want to consider the subject of mortality—especially his.

"Don't speak like that!" I scolded him. "Please let's not talk about such things!" Even though both of my parents had suffered from three separate bouts of cancer each, they had ultimately triumphed over their illnesses. Mercifully, they had come through every time and had hung in there, and I just couldn't bear to think that one day they *would* die.

"No, I really mean it," my father insisted, continuing his spiel. "When I die, I'm going to come back as a cardinal and comfort you."

Over the next few years, he became frailer. Eventually, he had to leave the house on Long Island in which he had lived for fifty years and relocate to an assisted-living residence in Boston, where many members of our family were located (I live in nearby Vermont). My mother had just died, and there was no one left at home to care for him, so this was the best option.

When my father had a stroke a year before he died, we realized that he would never be returning to Long Island, and one of my brothers went to his house and got it ready to sell. When my brother started to clean it out, I told him: "Make sure to save my book! The one about the cardinal." It represented the deep connection between my father and me, and the conversation we had after he read it remained vividly etched in my heart.

It hurt me to see how weak he had become. When he was eighty, lymphoma of the spleen had ravaged him. He had always been a strong, independent, and self-sufficient man, hearty and alive. Now he looked like an old man whose spirit had been erased. I was very sad.

My dad passed on a Monday. I drove home that night from Boston and collapsed into bed. The next morning, when I woke up, a deep heaviness lay on my heart. I had taken a day off from work; I was just too down to go in. I made myself a big cup of steaming coffee and held it in my hand as I absentmindedly gazed out the kitchen window. Just then, a cardinal appeared— seemingly out of nowhere—and landed on a branch just inches from the windowpane; it peered inside. It seemed to be staring at *me*. "Oh, look how beautiful it is!" was my first reaction, and then, "How unusual, that a cardinal would come so close when they are usually shy or scared of people."

Suddenly I remembered the pledge my father had made all those years ago: that he was going to come back as a cardinal and bring me comfort, and that memory unleashed more tears.

A few seconds later, the female cardinal (male and female cardinals, who mate for life, have different coloration, so it is easy to figure out their gender) joined him on the branch, and now *both* seemed to be looking directly at me!

I started crying and said, "Oh, Mom! Oh, Pop!" and the cardinals remained on the branch for a very long time—much longer than normal (as a bird-watcher I know that cardinals tend to flit frequently from place to place and never stay rooted anywhere for any significant amount of time). But in this case, it was different. They lingered near the kitchen window looking at me, not moving for what seemed like a small eternity. I had no problem believing that it was my parents whose spirits had come to visit and that they were very much with me.

I lived in that apartment for about four years, and those same cardinals were always there, either perched on the telephone wires above my house or singing in the backyard. It almost seemed as if they had adopted my residence as their own. Even the neighbors noticed how often they came to visit and expressed their amazement. One neighbor who often walked by would stop and say, in an awed tone, "Those cardinals are *always* there—in your backyard only, and no one else's!"

Most of the time I'd shrug my shoulders or smile, but say nothing. How could I tell people that I thought that my deceased parents were now birds? Surely they'd think that I was weird. But whenever I would go out to the garden, the cardinals would suddenly appear out of the blue, and the neighbors whom I *had* taken into my confidence would also notice the coincidence and continuously joke: "There are your folks!"

"Those cardinals really like you!" said one unsuspecting neighbor to whom I had not divulged my "secret" when she glanced into my garden on a sunny afternoon. "They are always out in the yard whenever you are. And they don't stop singing."

I knew they were singing to me, comforting me, and watching over me just as my parents had always done.

When I bought a house and moved thirteen miles away, I was sure that this would be the end of my cardinal "sightings." Cardinals don't usually migrate far, although it's not impossible.

But the day that I moved into my new digs, I went into the backyard and, sure enough, there they were: a pair of cardinals! I have no idea if they were the same birds as my previous visitors (other than the gender differences, cardinals don't have any distinguishing marks that set them apart), but I definitely felt that whoever they were, they contained the same spirits: my parents'.

These cardinals continue to come and visit frequently—not quite as often as the first pair did—but they definitely do seem to appear whenever I need some kind of comfort or guidance. And just like the first pair (*if* they are a new one), they don't shy away but come straight up to my window ledge and peer inside inquisitively. And they tend to stay for long periods of time.

Anyone who possesses an extensive knowledge of birds knows that this behavior from cardinals—coming up quite close to a human, and staying for an extended period of time— is highly unusual. They're not like chickadees, which have no problem approaching people and eating straight out of your hand. Cardinals are typically much more distant and aloof.

But not the ones that visit me. Two weeks ago, I came home from work, and there were the cardinals on my window ledge peering in, almost looking questioningly. I waved cheerfully and said "Hi, Mom and Dad. I'm OK, and it's so nice to see you!"

Naturally, I don't tell everyone this story, but perhaps the readers of this book will understand.

~ *Dot Lenhart*

MIRACLES

*M*iriam Perlstein was one of eight siblings who survived Auschwitz. It was so unusual for a family of eight—seven sisters and one brother—to emerge intact from the notorious death camp that when they landed on Ellis Island after the war, they became a media sensation. Repeatedly photographed and interviewed, they were besieged by reporters who wanted to know: *How was this possible? What made you so unique? Practically everyone else's family was decimated. Most of the survivors who limped into the New World had lost parents, children, spouses, siblings. But for an entire family of eight to have survived and found each other! How could it happen?*

"Miracles," the siblings answered patiently to everyone who asked.

And it was true. Miracles had abounded in all of their lives during their incarceration at Auschwitz, but Miriam's, they agreed, was vastly different from those experienced by Esther, Fanny, Bertha, Rose, Eva, Monci, and Binyamin. While their miracles fell under the realm of what could be called the rational, Miriam's belonged to a different category altogether.

Several weeks after her arrival at Auschwitz—after having survived several "selections" and having kept death at bay—sixteen-year-old Miriam was suddenly pulled out of the row of prisoners lining up for roll call one morning and transported to a separate section of the camp where a different procession was in place. Perhaps something about Miriam's demeanor that day had displeased the Nazi soldier whose gaze had settled upon her, or perhaps there was simply a quota to fill. For whatever random reason that no one could ever explain (and was there an explanation, after all, for the Nazis' haphazard and merciless decrees?), Miriam had been directed to join the column of prisoners marching slowly toward the crematorium that would turn them into ash.

At first, Miriam thought that she might have been sent on a new work detail. But the women in front of her and the women behind disabused her of that notion.

"Isn't there anything we can do?" she begged them.

"Look around you," they whispered. "Nazi soldiers with guns everywhere. How can we possibly escape?"

Miriam looked at where the women pointed. Unlike them, however, she didn't see the menacing guards with their drawn guns, nor the German shepherds who herded the pitiful tatters to their inevitable fate. What she saw instead at the corner of a building . . . several yards from where she stood . . . was the thoroughly unexpected but utterly beloved visage of her mother, Helen Perlstein, who had been transported with her daughters to Auschwitz and then transferred to a different barracks somewhere else. All these weeks, the daughters hadn't had any contact with their mother and couldn't find her. What was she doing *here*, of all places, Miriam wondered, right near the crematorium, and why were the soldiers oblivious to her presence? It was an incongruous emotion, to be sure, but even as she trudged toward certain death, Miriam's heart exploded with joy to see her mother again. But why was her head not shaved like everybody else's?

As Miriam studied her mother, in shock and bewilderment, her mother raised a scrawny arm, motioning that she should join her. Miriam glanced meaningfully at the guards nearby. *I can't*, she signaled with her eyes. Her mother nodded her head encouragingly and beckoned her again. *How could her mother think that she could escape?*

Miriam waved her hand at the soldiers who flanked her. *It's impossible*, her movements said. But suddenly there was a commotion in the back of the procession, and several guards dropped behind to investigate. *Now!* her mother gesticulated wildly. It made no sense, she was doomed to fail, but Miriam obeyed her mother's command. She broke from the line and ran toward her mother, who continued to gesture as she moved behind the building . . . but when Miriam turned the corner, her mother had vanished. Confused but emboldened, Miriam quickly ran for her life back to her barracks, back to where her sisters had been tensely waiting and now plied her with kisses and extra crusts of day-old bread.

"What happened to you?" they demanded. "Where did they take you? Where did you go?"

She told them everything: how her mother had astonishingly appeared at the precise place where she and the others had been rounded up, how the Nazis had been oddly unaware of her mother's presence, how she had insistently pantomimed that Miriam should run. "And I was so overjoyed to see Mamma again!" she babbled almost incoherently, still dazed by her experience. "She looked exactly as she always looked; they didn't even shave her head!"

The other sisters looked at one another wordlessly. They too were shaken by Miriam's recital: her brush with death made them shudder in fear, but it was their mother's intercession that made them tremble in awe.

"Miriam," one of them said gently, tenderly caressing her cheek to soften the blow. "We didn't want to tell you before, because you're the most sensitive among us. But we received reliable reports from several different prisoners working at the crematorium. Mamma was killed the first day she arrived, weeks ago."

"But I saw her clearly," Miriam wept. "If she hadn't signaled me to escape, I never would have tried."

~ Hindy Rosenberg, as told to the authors

PRETTY BIRD

A few short months after my father, Seymour Raven, died, I was engaged in a conversation on my car phone with my younger brother, Marc, whose wife was pregnant with their third child, which they knew via amniocentesis was a daughter. The topic under discussion with Marc was what they would name the baby. As Jewish tradition requires, children are named after deceased forebears (both male and female), often through the use of the first initial.

The conversation took some time, and since one of their other children had been named with the initial *S* for her other late grandfather, finding another acceptable name that began with *S* was, according to my brother, a daunting task. So daunting, it seemed, that they were seriously considering not naming the baby after my father at all. And this, we all knew, would be highly controversial and probably hurtful.

The conversation, in fact, lasted longer than the drive to my office, and though I had reached my destination, I remained in my parked car for some time while my brother and I continued to talk.

One of the names under consideration was Shana, which is the Hebrew word for "pretty." The problem, my brother explained to me, was that Shana Raven would, in a real sense, translate into "pretty bird," an image that troubled my brother and his wife because it seemed just a bit too cute.

To the contrary, I told my brother, it would be a warm remembrance. But he was troubled by this "little bird" image, and said so. As my brother related his misgivings about honoring my father's memory with a name that seemed to him somewhat contrived, I sat in my parked car and gazed, rather impatiently, out the windshield, at nothing in particular, thinking about how naming a daughter with the image of a "pretty bird" was not objectionable in the least, especially if it honored the memory of our recently departed father.

I have never believed in the Afterlife, although, in the days after my father's death, I had more than a few occasions to seek the sensation of his presence. And certainly discussing how to commemorate his life through a new life comes as close as one can to invoking his life force, in a real or imagined sense.

And then I froze; something that I had never once experienced took place, and it had a pronounced physical impact on me. A small, pretty bird of an unidentifiable species—truly unlike any I had seen before—landed on the hood of my car and sat there looking at me, not for a second, but for the longest time. It did not move. It simply perched on the hood and watched me as I spoke with my brother. My entire body tingled, and almost speechless, with a tear in my eye and a quavering voice, I told my brother why their soon-to-be-born daughter should be named Shana Raven. (And she is a pretty little bird, at that.)

~ *Jonathan Raven*

SHOPPING WITH SHOSHANA

She was more than just "my aunt."

My mom lives six hundred miles away from me, my mother-in-law eight hundred. My aunt Shoshana Schur, may she rest in peace, lived a cozy two blocks away, which, as I joked, gave me "all the advantages of a having a mom without the disadvantages." We both referred to her as "my local mom." Whenever Shoshana and my mother, Ema, were together in my presence, I'd always comment about "my biological mom and my local mom—in the same room!" My mother didn't mind. Shoshana was her sister, and Ema couldn't have been more thrilled with my choice of "adopted" mother.

One of our favorite activities was shopping together. Shoshana had an uncanny ability—and perpetual desire—to pick out the right clothes for everyone. "This would be just perfect for your niece, no?" she'd ask, holding up something nice—and, of course, for an unbelievable price. For years and years she'd do more shopping for others than for herself. "I thought this was your taste," she'd tell me—and whatever was in her hand was perfect. Shoshana even picked out a dress for her own future daughter-in-law—*before they'd even met*. And as always, it was spot-on: taste, size, and all. She matched clothes to people as successfully as she matched couples in her part-time career (and full-time obsession) as a matchmaker. *This* dress for her granddaughter, *that* for her daughter-in-law, that for my mother. . . . Her bargains fill all our closets. Always giving, always looking out for others. It wasn't just shopping with Shoshana—it was a lesson in generosity, in thoughtfulness, in putting others before herself.

She was barely sixty when cancer invaded. And won, despite her every effort to fight it off. From traditional medicine to experimental to alternative—you name it, she tried it. She knew there was so much left for her to do. Whether it be the many singles she was trying to fix up, or the kids she taught in Hebrew school who still needed her to bring Judaism to life for them, or the guests she wanted to continue hosting as she had for decades in her "open house"—Shoshana really wanted to live. And she gave it her all.

Toward the end, when she was too uncomfortable for company, I kept my visits short. But I kept one running joke going. "You gotta get well," I'd tell her as I had from the very beginning of her illness. "I just can't go to the Lord & Taylor Clearance Center myself!"

The serious stuff—losing my local mom, having my kids lose their "Grandma Chicago" before they'd hardly even gotten to know her . . . not having her advice about everything under the sun . . . not seeing her dance at her youngest son's wedding . . . all that, we knew would be devastating. And I obviously wasn't going to upset her by bringing that up. I didn't even want to think about it. But it was the trivial stuff that kept coming to my mind, and even made me laugh a bit through my tears.

I imagined myself without her at the Lord & Taylor Clearance Center, our favorite hangout—and I didn't like the picture. I'd walk in all alone, then memories would flood my mind and I'd snap. "Security to Main Entrance," I'd hear over the loudspeaker just before some guard would haul me out. . . . Or else, if I were strong enough to make it inside, something would trigger a memory, and I'd collapse on the floor in tears as curious shoppers passed by. "See, I just lost my aunt. . . . She'd come here with me all the time . . ." I'd babble on tearfully as they tsk-tsk'd in sympathy. The image made me laugh, as horrible as it was. So I'd always make a comment about the Clearance Center when I visited, hoping to make her smile too.

Near the end, I went in for one of my short visits. "Hi again," I said, taking her hand. "It's your Clearance partner."

"Is that," she said, though it was quite difficult for her to speak at that point, "all you're going to remember me for?"

"Oh, noooo," I said, trying to make her smile. "Syms too."

It didn't work.

She didn't even smirk. I guess she didn't appreciate humor at that stage. So then I went on a little, telling her there was much more: how her matchmaking skills helped me get married because she realized I was head over heels in love with the man who is now my husband before I myself realized it. . . . And how she hosted us for several weeks when, as newlyweds, our apartment wasn't ready. . . . We'd have breakfast in her "hotel," go to the apartment during the day, and come back to our luxury "suite" in the evening, with dinner waiting for us. And how I couldn't imagine myself hosting someone for that long! How she picked up my kids—her "Chicago grandchildren"—for synagogue every Sabbath, and gave me practical advice when they were in some stage or another that I was having trouble with. . . . She could give great advice even while she was so sick. I guess she enjoyed discussing something besides cancer, doctors, and medicine.

It was a few days after Passover when we lost her. I'm sure, in her continuous tradition of putting others before herself, she didn't want to ruin our holiday and begged the Angel of Death to hold off so the yearly anniversary wouldn't fall on Passover. I could picture the scene of her effective argument very clearly. She had used the same tone of voice to convince me of so many things.

Her son had notified me that her passing was imminent, so I was there when she died.

It's funny how, even though you know something awful is going to happen, it still destroys you when it does.

After hanging around the house in a daze for a while, I somehow walked home. It was 1:00 p.m., and I absently flipped through the mail that had just been delivered.

A familiar bright-yellow-and-black flyer caught my attention immediately.

"THE [CHICAGO] LORD & TAYLOR CLEARANCE CENTER" the big, bold lettering shouted at me, just two hours after Shoshana left this world, "IS HAVING A GOING-OUT-OF–BUSINESS SALE."

I didn't know whether to laugh or cry.

Did the Clearance Center decide it wasn't worth staying open without my aunt's patronage? Obviously not, but I smiled at the thought. . . . Or maybe it was something else altogether. . . .

Was it Shoshana laughing at me?

I could clearly picture her saying, "You didn't want to go to the Clearance Center without me?"

Then shrugging her shoulders and adding, ". . . so you *won't*!"

~ *Bina Simon*

DEBBY'S CHALLAH

When my mother told me she had been diagnosed with cancer, I never once thought she wouldn't get better. Even when she told me it was stage IV, even when I watched the chemo ravage her body, I always assumed that this would just be one of those down times in our family saga that we would one day look back on with sighs of relief.

If you'd known my mother, you'd understand why. She was one of those women with a superhuman capacity to do everything, do it well, and make it look easy. In between raising four children, working on and off, running our household (and the synagogue gift shop), and making sure a home-cooked dinner was on the table every night, my mother also hosted challah-baking classes in our kitchen every few months. (Challah is a special Jewish braided bread eaten on the Sabbath and holidays.) People clamored for a seat at our Sabbath table just for a warm, doughy slice of "Debby's Challah," and her recipe was sought after by every woman within three zip codes. She gave leadership courses to corporate executives across the country, taught preschool in the inner city, and threw parties people talked about for *years* afterward. Up against a woman like my mother, a pesky little thing like cancer didn't stand a chance.

But despite the aggressive treatment, the cancer spread too quickly for the doctors to catch up with it. She passed away a little more than a year after her diagnosis.

During the shiva, I heard something I had never heard before: "She should be a *melitzas yosher* for you and your family."

"What does that mean?" I asked my husband.

"It's like an advocate," he replied. "Someone who prays for mercy on your behalf in Heaven, and is your direct intermediary with God, interceding actively whenever necessary."

Before I tell you my reaction to this, allow me to give you a little background. Just a few years before, I had completely overturned my life to become an Orthodox Jew. I'd revamped my wardrobe, cleared my Saturday schedule, and reconstructed my fundamental philosophies of life. I'd come to live by dicta and beliefs that demanded me to stretch well beyond the bounds of logic, and, for the most part, I'd happily done so. I had learned about the *neshamah* (the higher soul) and *gilgul* (reincarnated soul), and it made sense to me. I even liked the idea of getting another turn at bat if you didn't quite make it around the bases the first time. But when I heard what my husband said, I just couldn't swallow it. He actually expected me to believe that my mother was in Heaven wheeling and dealing for me like some kind of fairy godmother?

This, by the way, was not because I doubted my mother's capacity to hold sway in the heavenly realms. In fact, if anyone could make waves up there, there was no one better qualified than she. When Mom was alive, nothing was more important to her than her family; if she sensed even a hint of a threat to our tight-knit little clan, she would immediately mobilize to snuff it out. And when it came to her children, Mom was a lioness. Once, when a classmate bullied me at school, my mother stared her down like a sniper as the poor girl walked from the school entrance to her carpool, quaking in her pink rain boots. If anyone could charge up to the heavenly throne and make a case for her kids, it was definitely Mom.

But I still didn't buy it. Even if it was true, how would anyone really know?

For the first couple of years after she died, my sister would occasionally tell me that she'd seen our mother in a dream, or had had some experience that was unmistakably linked to her. I heard the same thing from my aunt, who was my mother's best friend. I, however, could not commiserate. Wherever my mother was, the signal between there and here must not have been very good. Or, more likely, I thought, my family members just believed what they *wanted* to believe.

Not that I blamed them. I missed my mother terribly; I would have loved for something to happen that would dispel my skepticism and make it clear that she was on the Other Side, pulling strings for me. But from where I stood, the only connections I had left to her were my memories and the gaping hole in my life she'd left behind when she died.

Last year, my husband and I decided to move from our small, beloved out-of-town community to someplace more urban. We needed to be closer to my stepdaughters, who lived in the city, and we also wanted the Jewish resources that a larger community had to offer. We were going for all the right reasons, and although it would be an adjustment for everyone, we were confident that the move would ultimately be a good one.

Fast forward six months, and we were desperately struggling, particularly on the social and financial fronts. It wasn't working out as we'd hoped; we were isolated, without help, slipping deeper and deeper into debt and backed against the wall. We met with our rabbi, who advised us to move, but we had no idea where to, or how we would even afford it.

One night not long after our meeting, an e-mail popped up on my phone, seemingly out of nowhere: it was a job listing for something I'd wanted to do for a number of years, but had never known how to pursue. The compensation included a house and utilities. *There's got to be some kind of catch*, I thought as I typed in my response.

Not ten minutes later I got a call back. I chatted with the woman who would be my supervisor, just waiting for some kind of red flag signaling that the job wouldn't be a good fit. But the hours were perfect. The location was great. (I'd grown up ten minutes away from where we would live, and I knew the community well; I'd even have family nearby!) And the job itself seemed tailor-made for me: honestly, I thought, feeling the tiniest flutter of excitement in my belly, if this job was as good as it sounded, I would have paid *her* to let me do it. But, I reminded myself, I hadn't seen the house yet. I had just had my third baby; we would need something that would accommodate everyone.

The day I went to meet with her and see the place, I braced myself for disappointment. It just seemed too good to be true. But as I walked into the house, I gasped. It wasn't fancy, but it was lovely. Cozy. Perfect for me and my family. Looking around at the light-filled rooms, I could see us living here, and happily.

A week passed, and the call finally came: the job was mine. We had six weeks to pack up a house we'd moved into only six months before, only this time we had to do it with a two-month-old baby—in addition to his three-year-old and five-year-old brothers. It was harrowing, overwhelming, and completely exhausting. More than once, up to my neck in cardboard boxes, I questioned whether we would make it to moving day.

Little did I know, our six-week crunch turned out to be training for the Olympics. The move was even tougher than the packing. There were endless delays, the kids were restless, and when time started running short, the movers almost left all of our things on the sidewalk until my husband convinced them to finish.

Thankfully, we managed to get everything into the house in time, but it was thrown in haphazardly; when the movers left, it looked as if a hurricane had torn through the place. My husband and I dug out two mattresses from the labyrinth of furniture, put the boys to bed, and stared at each other in complete disbelief, like two survivors after a plane crash.

Exhausted, I wandered into the kitchen, the only room with space to move. I absently opened the cabinets and drawers, trying to get an idea of how to organize. They were all empty, as expected, except for one cupboard, down next to the oven. Inside was a small card, a piece of stationery with pictures of vegetables on the margin. There was something written on the preprinted lines, and I picked up the card to read it.

It was a recipe: *4½ cups flour, ⅔ cups sugar, 2 pkgs. yeast . . .* This list looked familiar. Where had I seen it before?

Then I looked at the top of the card. *Recipe for,* said the template. And written on the line next to it: *Debby's Challah.*

I felt the hairs rise on the back of my neck.

It was *my mother's* challah recipe.

"Oh, my gosh . . . ," I whispered.

In that instant, my mind flashed through the last few months: The unexpected crisis. The even more unexpected rescue. The amazing job. The perfect house. The community right near where I grew up. And now this.

There was no question, even for a confirmed skeptic like me, that she had done this for me. My mother had been my *melitzas yosher.* And she'd even sent me a little something just so I'd know.

To be honest, it shouldn't have surprised me. It was just like her to pull off something like this.

"Well," I smiling at my husband across our landscape of boxes, "I guess we're home."

~ *Rea Bochner*

THE BORROWED BOOK

*R*abbi Mendel Brachfeld was considered one of the outstanding Orthodox Jewish sages of the late twentieth century. He was also known as a man of great personal integrity who possessed the highest standards of ethics. My father-in-law of blessed memory, Rabbi Leibl Mandelbaum, considered himself privileged to have a close relationship with Mendel, whom he regarded as both his mentor and his friend.

Mendel predeceased my father-in-law by several years, but even in the Next World, it seemed, he couldn't quite concentrate on heavenly matters until he had successfully settled his more earthly concerns. One night, long after he had soared to the celestial spheres, Mendel descended to mortal realms to relay an urgent message to his friend in Antwerp, Shaul Hutterer.

"Shaul!" he exclaimed, appearing to his old friend in a dream. "You have to do me a favor. I borrowed a holy book from someone and never had a chance to return it before I passed away. Please make sure that the *sefer* [volume of religious writings] is returned to the rightful owner." And then he vanished.

Shaul awoke from the dream deeply shaken, but also somewhat vexed. If Mendel had managed to come all the way from the Other World, couldn't he have at least given him some additional information? Like the *name* of the holy book, for instance, or the *name* of the man to whom it belonged? And why did Mendel need him to serve as intermediary? Couldn't he have simply appeared in the dream of the man who had loaned him the book to begin with? *But who am I to question the ways of the Other Side?* Shaul chastised himself. He took the dream seriously; he didn't think it was the result of the day's detritus, a hallucination, or the random meanderings of a sleeping brain. He did believe that he'd received a visitation. But as awe-inspiring as it was to receive a little tap from beyond this world, he couldn't help but be a trifle annoyed.

Who knew how many holy books Mendel had owned in his lifetime and left behind or how many jostled for pride of place in his imposing bookcase, which spanned the length of his living room wall? How could he possibly locate the right one, the one that Mendel had obliquely referenced in his dream? With so little to go on, the actual possibility of tracking it down seemed remote. Nonetheless, Shaul had been given an important task, and he knew that Mendel would not be able to rest until the holy book was returned. So Shaul picked up the phone and dutifully called Mendel's son in New York. He waited for a sigh of exasperation or frustration to come from the other end. After all, with the heavenly communiqué he had been assigned to convey, Shaul was about to dispatch Rabbi Brachfeld's son on what would probably be a wild goose chase. But to his surprise, Mr. Brachfeld's son was neither skeptical about the dream nor phased by the daunting task with which his deceased father had charged his friend.

"Of course!" his son immediately leaped to the right conclusion. "I'm sure I know who my father means. His friend Leibl Mandelbaum, a true bibliophile and religious scholar, was constantly recommending—and always loaning—my father new religious books to read. I bet it's a *sefer* that belongs to him."

Mr. Brachfeld started rummaging among his father's vast collection of holy books and, sure enough, unearthed a volume in which "Leibl Mandelbaum" was inscribed. When it was returned to my father-in-law, he was delighted and overwhelmed by surprise. "I had no idea what had become of the *sefer*!" my father-in-law, somewhat of an absentminded genius himself, said.

A few years later, my father-in-law was called to the Other World, and this story was recounted at his funeral by his nephew in order to demonstrate both his unusual erudition and the kind of illustrious company he kept. The next day, when my husband was sitting shiva, one of my father-in-law's peers came to pay his respects, bearing a gift.

"Here," he said, pulling a well-worn volume from a plastic shopping bag. "This is a *sefer* I borrowed from your father, and I want to return it immediately."

"Thank you very much," my husband said, a little confused by the man's breach of etiquette, "but you didn't have to bring it now—to the shiva."

"What . . . are you kidding?" the man looked at my husband with alarm. "I heard the story at the funeral about Mendel Brachfeld and the *sefer* he borrowed from your father. Do you think I want your father to come to me in my dreams? Take it . . . please!" And he practically shoved the holy book into my husband's hands and fled.

~ *Yitta Halberstam*

METAMORPHOSIS

In 1966, a distraught Jewish father from Tel Aviv, Israel, approached Rabbi Shlomo Carlebach, popularly known as "The Singing Rabbi"—a charismatic leader renowned for his outreach to hundreds of thousands of seekers—and appealed to him for help.

"Please, can you try to get through to my son? He is a high officer in the army, and he may very well be a proud Israeli, but he's *not* a proud Jew. He just hates, really hates religious Jews. This has been going on for some time, but now he has a new kind of craziness. In my house, in my dining room, there hangs a big picture of my deceased grandfather, an Orthodox Jew with a long beard and a fur hat. My son said that unless I take down that picture he refuses to come to my house. He said it is nauseating to him to think he is the grandson of such an idiot! What should I do with him?"

Rabbi Carlebach tried very hard to persuade the young officer to respect his father's traditions and not cause him undue anguish, but the son was defiant and inflexible. Unlike his father, who wore a yarmulke to signify his observance, the officer's head was bare. He did not keep the Jewish laws, and he remained adamant that the painting be removed. "He had some kind of block against religion," Rabbi Carlebach later told his friends, Dr. Joshua Ritchie and Liliane Ritchie, who continue to recount the story today. "I just didn't know what to do."

Shlomo simply could not prevail upon the young man to change his ways, and eventually he gave up trying.

One year later, in 1967, after Israel emerged triumphant from the Six-Day War, the door to Rabbi Carlebach's home in the Israeli settlement of Mevo Modi'im in Israel suddenly opened, and in walked the father, accompanied by his son the officer—now wearing the full regalia of an ultra-Orthodox Jew—a little beard, side curls, and prayer fringes poking out from underneath his garments. "He looked like an entirely new person," the Ritchies remember Rabbi Carlebach reporting to them. He was astonished by the metamorphosis.

"What happened to you?" Shlomo asked the officer.

This is the story the young man told:

"During the Six-Day War, I was driving a tank in Sinai. Suddenly, I saw an Egyptian tank on my tail, followed by others, and I was trying to get as close as possible to the other Israeli tanks because I knew I couldn't fight a bunch of Egyptian tanks all by myself. So I was driving as fast as I could, when suddenly I saw an old Jew, wearing a *tallit* (prayer shawl) and *tefillin* in the middle of the road . . . praying! I couldn't believe my eyes! And you know what I think about religious Jews, that they are crazy! I knew they were crazy, but *that* crazy, in the middle of a war? And here in the desert, standing, *praying*?

"My first reaction was: 'I should really run him over.' But how can you run over another human being? So I made a detour. The Egyptian tank driver, however, the one who was following me, didn't have any such compunction, didn't make a detour, and drove right over the place where the old Jew had been standing. And *boom!* It was blown up by a mine that had been buried under the ground on exactly the spot toward which I myself had been headed, had I not swerved to avoid hitting the elderly man. I had the chills. I looked back to see what had happened to the Jew, but he was gone. Where could he have disappeared to in such a short time? Could he too have been killed? Or had he stepped away from the spot, just in the nick of time? I wondered uneasily about his fate, but the inevitable skirmish with the other Egyptian tanks in which I became engaged consumed all my attention.

"When I later visited my father and came to his house in Tel Aviv, I noticed the picture of my grandfather, which he had *not* taken down, after all. I had never really paid much attention to it, because it had grossed me out. But now goose bumps erupted all over my body. Because peering at it closely for the first time in my life, I saw clearly that this was the same man who had stood in the desert praying, the man who had saved my life! But my grandfather was long dead . . . I had never even met him. How could this be? I was stunned. The man in the desert had not been a mirage, I knew. So there was only one possible explanation. My grandfather had made a *very* long journey—he had come all the way down from Heaven—to save me, his recalcitrant grandson, now a true believer!"

~ *Shlomo Carlebach, as told to Joshua and Liliane Ritchie*

A MESSAGE FOR MARION

I'm the oldest of eight siblings. When I was ten years old, over twenty years ago, my youngest sister, Lily, passed away suddenly. It was tragic, but I was young, and as life moved forward, I found myself dwelling on the loss less and less. Yet there's something I've learned: time moves on, pain is dulled, but you never, ever forget. I'm now married with six kids, but my story begins almost three years ago, when I had five.

One night, I was in bed asleep when I found myself in that limbo, in-between stage where you've kind of just woken up, but not really; you're still asleep, but not sound asleep. My eyelids were heavily closed; nonetheless I suddenly knew with absolute certainty that there was someone else in the room. And I knew it wasn't my husband—he leaves for work in the early pre-dawn hours, long before I'm awake—and it was clear that he was already gone. Was it an intruder? I felt paralyzed with fear. I thought: "Someone's in here. Who is it?" and I heard an answer in my head, "Lily."

I don't know about other people, but stories about ghosts, spirits, or visits from the Other World make my skin prickle and all the little hairs on my arms stand up on end. I find no comfort in thinking that someone I can't see is watching me; I find it creepy! But I was too scared to sit up and open my eyes, frightened by what I might find. At least if I stayed in my sleeping position, I could pretend that it was just a bizarre dream.

"I have a message for Marion," I heard in my head. Marion is my sister; she was four when Lily passed away.

"Fine," I said.

I heard her say. "Please tell her that everything will be OK."

"OK. But next time, if you have a message for her, please tell her yourself. In a few minutes, I'm going to wake up, and I'm going to be completely freaked out."

I don't remember any longer how I actually felt when I opened my eyes, if I was spooked or anything, but I do remember thinking that Marion would never believe me. Hey, if it hadn't happened to me, I don't know if I would have believed it either.

A few days later, I still hadn't told anyone, least of all Marion, who was overseas at the time. Then, finally I decided this: I know it happened. I was given a message, so I should pass it on. If she laughs at me, oh well, at least I did what I was supposed to do.

I picked up the phone and called Marion. I told her, "I know you're not going to believe me, but . . . ," and I told her. I waited for Marion's laughter but heard a sniff instead.

"Are you there?" I asked.

"Yes." She was crying.

Once she calmed down a bit, she told me, "That's just what I needed to hear."

I didn't probe, but I felt very validated. I knew it had happened!

"I told Lily to go directly to you next time she has a message for you," I told Marion.

"Oh, no," she said, "I would totally lose it." (It's true—she's very sensitive.)

A few weeks later, I found out what was going on in Marion's life. She'd been dating someone and needed some kind of sign that everything would be fine. Lily's reassurance came at just the right time, and soon afterward, Marion and the young man she had been dating celebrated their engagement. Today Marion is happily married.

A few months after Marion's wedding, I found out I was expecting again. I had four sons and one daughter and—I'm not embarrassed to say this—I was absolutely dying for another baby girl. I know you have to say that whatever God gives you, you'll be happy with . . . and it's true, ultimately. But I still really wanted that baby girl, pink and purple and ruffles and frills and cuddles! I planned to find out the gender at my twenty-week ultrasound because if it was to be another boy, I'd need time to get used to the idea. I was on tenterhooks.

Soon after I discovered I was pregnant, the same dream scenario occurred once again. Lily came to visit a second time. The circumstances were exactly the same: I was roused from sleep, I was alone in the room, and I felt the deep sense that someone else was there with me. Actually, this time I felt like there were two people present. I can't explain why I felt that way. I just did.

"Someone's here. Who is it?" I thought in my head.

"Lily." No acknowledgment of the second soul. "I have a message for you and for Marion."

"No, thanks. If you have a message for Marion, please go tell her yourself."

"OK."

"Wait!" I suddenly thought in my head. "Before you go, am I having a girl or a boy?"

"It's a girl."

When I woke up, I felt at peace. A girl! Yay! Thank you, God!

And then I thought: Uh-oh. What was the *message*? Oh, I'm such a twit. Maybe there will be something wrong with the baby and she came to warn me.

Marion was also very miffed with me that I hadn't been willing to be the vessel for *her* message.

For the rest of my pregnancy, I continuously worried about my baby's health. I was convinced there would be something wrong. I prayed a lot. I was also too scared to sleep alone in my room anymore after my husband left for work.

In July 2013, my baby girl was born, healthy and perfect, thank God. She felt familiar. Perhaps it was she who had accompanied Lily when she came to visit that night when I was in the early stages of my pregnancy? I definitely felt Lily had had a second soul in tow. But unless Lily comes again to visit and verifies my suspicions, I'll never know for sure.

As for the messages she wanted to relay to both me and Miriam, which I absolutely refused to hear, they remain a tantalizing mystery.

~ Anonymous, as told to the authors

A PROPHETIC DREAM

Throughout my difficult childhood, my paternal grandparents, who lived two blocks away during my preteen years, and then a few miles away until their passing, were my sanctuary. They were the center of stability for me—the people I turned to when I needed reassurance, love, support. They were not wealthy by any means, except for what mattered: kindness, compassion, love. Without them, I'm not sure I would have survived childhood.

I spoke with my grandparents nearly every day, and after I married and had children my grandfather was my on-call babysitter. I wouldn't even have to ask. He'd pick up the phone and say, "What time?" My grandparents also had dinner with us once a week. I can still hear my grandpa's voice in my head as he entered our home. "How do? How do?" he'd say and gather his great-grandchildren into his arms, then kiss me on the cheek.

In April 2000, as I was preparing our weekly dinner, I received a phone call from my grandma. "Grandpa walked into the edge of a wall last night. He's in bad shape. Can you come over?"

I dropped everything and was at their apartment in ten minutes.

When I arrived, Grandpa was in bed, nearly unrecognizable. His left eye was swollen shut, his face black and blue.

Swallowing panic, I picked up the phone and called my best friend's husband, who was an ophthalmologist. He just happened to be home that late afternoon, a small miracle. I described Grandpa's condition and he came right over.

"I wish he'd go to the hospital," the eye doctor told me after examining Grandpa, "but he's adamant about staying home." He gave me some prescriptions to fill, which I did immediately.

The next morning at around five o'clock, I bolted awake from a disturbing dream, a dream so real I immediately burst into tears. In the dream, I found myself walking into a hospital room. My grandpa was in bed, surrounded by deceased relatives, several of whom I recognized as his brothers and sisters. Other than my grandpa, I was the only "living" person in the room.

I came to his bedside and said, "I'm sorry, Grandpa. I'm sorry."

To this day, I can conjure his voice and hear how emphatic he was with his answer. "Forget about it. Don't worry about it." He lifted his hand as if to wave my concerns away. When I woke up, I couldn't think of one reason why I had to ask for forgiveness. It disturbed me. My only comfort was his strong dismissal of my apology.

The dream continued. I remember looking around at the ethereal visitors. I was profoundly aware of the "family" surrounding him, and I wanted Grandpa's reassurance and comfort that he was going to be fine. Shifting my gaze to Grandpa, I saw that his eyes were closed. A small, peaceful smile graced his angelic face. A moment later, his departed loved ones left, and I stood alone with his body.

The experience seemed so real, I was certain it had happened. It took me a few seconds to get reoriented to my surroundings.

Upon hearing my sobs, my husband, Jim, woke up. "What's the matter?" he asked. I told him about the dream.

"I have to see if he's all right! I have to call my grandma."

"If something happened, you know she'd call you," he reassured me. But I couldn't shake off the fear and trepidation. "They're probably still sleeping. Wait until eight o'clock. You don't want to worry them."

Torn over what to do, I listened to Jim's reasoning and watched the clock. At exactly eight, I called.

The second Grandma picked up, I asked, "Is Grandpa OK?"

"I need you. I can't take care of him myself," she said, sounding so frantic I grabbed my keys and raced to the door. Relief washed over me, too. At least he was alive. I wasn't too late. Everything would be fine. I took the dream as a warning, one I prayed I could prevent from coming true.

Time stopped and sped up. I have no recollection of what happened between the call and my arrival at their apartment.

Once again, I found Grandpa in bed and Grandma trying to soothe him. With one glance, I knew we had to get him to the hospital immediately. Before I could hit the 9 in 911, Grandpa protested with a fury I had never heard from him before. "No! I do *not* want to go to any hospital," he yelled.

I slinked out of the room and, with tears in my eyes, called the eye doctor. "He's much worse," I said. "But he refuses to go to the hospital. I don't know what to do. I can't go against his wishes."

"Let me speak to him," he said.

I walked into my grandparents' bedroom. "Grandpa," I said, "the doctor wants to speak to you." I handed him an extension and headed back to the dining room with the other phone pressed to my ear.

With a gentle but firm touch, the doctor explained why it was critical for Grandpa to go to the hospital. "I need you to agree," he said. Finally, Grandpa mumbled what I was pretty sure was a yes. We hung up and I dialed 911.

When the EMTs arrived, Grandpa flew into a rage again. "I told you," he said to me, "that I don't want to go!" My heart ripped open. Guilt covered me like a violent summer storm. A part of me felt that I had tricked him into agreeing to go and had made the doctor the fall guy.

As the EMTs worked on my grandpa, he calmed down. I not only saw him sigh, resigned to his fate, but felt it through my body. I knew I had taken a choice away from him. I had wrenched from him control over a decision he had thought was his: to remain in his home. I silently repeated that it was for the best. That I had done the right thing, that his health came first.

I followed the ambulance to the hospital. Once my grandpa was situated, I joined him in the emergency room. Needing to reassure both of us, I said, "Grandpa, you're going to be OK. You have great doctors looking out for you. They will take excellent care of you."

He answered, "The doctors are wonderful human beings. But this is between me and God."

Tears streamed down my face, and I was profoundly grateful his eyes were closed. There was nothing I could say in response.

Once Grandpa was admitted, I put the dream aside, along with the possibility of him dying. I had to, because in two days I would be co-chairing an auction to raise money for breast cancer research. Months and months of hard work had gone into planning the event. My grandparents knew all about it, and had even solicited items. Without any doubt, I knew they were vested in the auction's success for my sake.

A day after Grandpa was admitted to the hospital, he called, sounding so upbeat and cheerful I thought he was on the road to recovery. After some small talk, his voice grew serious, so serious that it gave me pause. "When's your auction?" he asked.

"Tomorrow night," I said.

"What time does it end?"

"Should be done by eleven."

He took a deep breath. "You'll do great. It'll be the best event ever." Then he hung up. Later, after I thought about how he specifically asked me when the auction would end, I came to the conclusion that Grandpa knew he was dying and was holding on until I was finished with my responsibilities. He always put others first, especially family.

True to his words, we raised more money that year than any previous year. Ecstatic, I walked on clouds and went to sleep with exhausted satisfaction. The dream from two days before was pretty much forgotten.

In the morning, I drove the kids to school and came home to shower. As I dressed, the phone rang. A dread engulfed me. It was the hospital.

"Jack passed away," a nurse informed me. "Your grandma is here, and your aunt and uncle are coming in from Janesville if you want to come, too."

Scrambling around, I found my shoes, jumped into the car, and sped toward the hospital. Flashing lights stopped my progress. When the officer came to my window, he asked me if I knew why I'd been pulled over. I shook my head. "You did a rolling stop," he said, "and kept going." Sobbing, I explained the circumstances. Sympathetic, he let me go with a gentle reminder to drive carefully. I heeded that warning.

"I want to see him," I said to Grandma, after a tearful greeting and hugs. My aunt led me to Grandpa's room but didn't come in. Like a bolt of lightning in a black sky, the dream streaked into my memory. Here I was walking into my grandpa's hospital room, just like before. Slowly, I made my way inside and stood next to his bed. I looked down. His angelic face held that beautiful, peaceful smile, exactly as I had remembered.

I knew, without any doubt, that Grandpa was content, surrounded by his siblings and loved ones. But guilt overshadowed my sense of peace. I knew I had forced him to go to the hospital when he didn't want to go. Once again, I asked for his forgiveness. His words echoed in my head, "Forget about it. Don't worry about it." And I knew he meant it.

As painful as it was to experience this prophetic dream, I'm also grateful. Knowing how Grandpa always put others first and the tight bond we shared, I felt that I had been with him at the end, at least in spirit. The warning and the vision and the forgiveness helped me cope with the deep loss. It was, in my mind, his last act of kindness, compassion, and, most of all, love.

~ *Liza Wiemer*

GIFTS FROM GRANDPA

After my beloved grandpa passed away, I was engulfed in a fog that I couldn't shake off. It followed me around like a shadow. I missed him so much. Even though he was eighty-eight years old when he died, it was way too soon. I needed him. He had always been a stable force throughout my difficult childhood and was a solid support throughout my adulthood.

When I was little, I frequently slept over at my grandparents'. He'd tuck me into bed and stay with me until I fell asleep, making me feel safe and loved. As an adult, when I was hospitalized for nearly a month, he held my hand and told me stories to keep my mind occupied so that I wouldn't dwell on the upcoming surgery I had to endure and the infections that followed. He babysat my children and would always tell me how perfectly they behaved, even though I'd find out later from my grandma that they weren't such angels. Every time I visited my grandparents at their apartment building and got buzzed inside, he greeted his great-grandchildren and me at the top of the stairs, so anxious to see us that he never waited inside. He showered us with hugs, kisses, *love.*

I missed that love the most.

A few weeks after he passed, Grandma asked me to clean out Grandpa's drawers and closet. I was struck speechless by the things he had saved and cherished. There were wedding announcements and invitations from his married grandchildren, clippings about his five great-grandchildren and nine grandchildren that had appeared in newspapers, detailing our accomplishments, and programs from school plays and activities.

He had next to nothing of material value to pass on, but the memories he valued showed he was a wealthy man indeed.

Still, I wanted some kind of memento to save, something to physically hold onto. But it did not seem there was anything "special" to take home. We donated all his clothes. After that, there was his wallet with his driver's license. I had his family Bible, but it wasn't something I could remember him holding or showing to me, other than the one day he gave it to me.

I did, however, have colorful napkins and scratchy toilet paper that Grandpa had received from a friend as a thank-you for driving this man around on errands. The man had a connection to some paper distributor, and he had a near endless supply of free "irregulars." In turn, Grandpa gave family and friends these necessities to keep our bums and faces clean. Whenever Grandpa came loaded, we laughed about it. To this day, I have a gallon-sized plastic bag with a few purple napkins labeled "From Grandpa." It's a humorous story and a symbol of his generosity that we'll pass on to other generations.

Still, toilet paper and napkins weren't cutting it for me. At the time, it was hard to explain why I felt so desperate for something physical to hold onto, other than wanting a connection to him. As I was to recognize later, what I really wanted, what I really needed, was to know he was still with me, watching over me. I needed something to soften the sting of the deep loss I couldn't shake.

Whenever the gloom became too much to bear, I would take a walk to Lake Michigan via Beach Drive, a hilly, winding road with magnificent homes and sparking sand about a mile and a half from my home. Once I reached the lake, I'd find a private boulder to sit on and stare out at the water until nature's beauty invigorated my soul and the heaviness was lifted a bit. At this point in my life, these walks were a near daily occurrence.

Until one day, when my plans to walk down to the beach changed. I had already started out and was thinking about my grandpa, praying for a sign that he was with me. In my head, I heard a voice say, "Don't walk down to the beach. Take your car."

My car? I wondered. Why would I take my car? But the urge was so strong that I turned around, walked back home, and got into my minivan.

As I descended the hill, I fought annoyance. Once I reached the beach, there was no place for me to park. At best, I'd be able to pull off to the side in a "No Parking" zone for few minutes. It hardly seemed like enough to soothe my foul mood and aching soul.

Then I saw the sign: the reason why I needed to take my car, instead of walking to the lake.

My grandpa's brother just happened to have a home on Beach Drive. For months and months I hadn't given my great-uncle's home much thought, other than to acknowledge the fact that he still owned it. He wasn't living there anymore. He had moved to an assisted-living facility, and his home had sat empty for quite a long time.

On this day, his home wasn't empty. Streams of people were entering it. There was a huge "Estate Sale" sign in the yard.

I pulled into the driveway, parked, and went inside.

Unlike my grandpa, this great-uncle was monetarily wealthy. I found tons of family mementos—books that had been inscribed with birthday greetings from my grandpa to his brother, table-cloths, and a few other knickknacks. I ended up purchasing quite a bit and loading up the car.

Obviously, I would have seen the estate sale if I had walked to the beach. But it would have been a huge inconvenience, and since it was late afternoon, I most likely wouldn't have made it home in time before they closed the sale. I also wouldn't have had my wallet. I never carried it on a walk.

I ended up giving many of the items I bought to other family members. I have a few of the books and a couple of table-cloths that had graced my great-aunt's table. These things hold very little monetary value, but instead are sentimental to me as a writer and someone who loves to cook and entertain.

Upon leaving my great-uncle's home, the fog that had been following me lifted. These "gifts" from Grandpa helped me come to terms with the physical loss. I look back on that moment and know it was his way of giving me what I needed: a sign that he was watching over me. Then and always.

~ *Liza Wiemer*

HEAVENLY BIRTHDAY WISHES

On September 23, 2009, I celebrated my first birthday without my beloved grandma. She had passed away ten months before, and I missed her profoundly. We were extremely close and talked nearly every day. Each phone call ended with her saying, "I love you," to which I always said, "I love you too." At ninety-four years young, those were the last words she mouthed to me before her soul left her body. Despite my sadness and loss, I felt grateful to have had her in my life for so long.

Birthdays and anniversaries were very important to my grandma. She never forgot one. She celebrated family's birthdays with cards mailed to arrive on the special day, and always, *always* there was a phone call to shower blessings upon us. Several days before other family members' birthdays or wedding anniversaries, she'd call to make sure I didn't forget to call and add my best wishes.

On this particular birthday, I had a profound ache in my heart. There would be no call, no card in the mail. I went to teach preschool in the morning with a heaviness that took away some of the joy from the day.

It quickly lifted when my co-teacher and students surprised me with flowers and a cake. That is, until I left school. Once again, the stabbing loss returned.

After teaching, I had planned to return some books to the library, followed by a stop at the grocery store. But because I had received the bouquet and it was an unseasonably warm day, I decided I didn't want to leave the flowers in the car to wilt. I headed home, which was about a mile from school, put the flowers in water, and debated whether to go to the grocery store first or the library. Logic said, "Go to the library, then the grocery store." It made sense. Why would I keep food in a warm car?

But a stronger voice compelled me to go the grocery store first. The library would only take a minute, so no foul for the groceries. I drove the four blocks to the store.

Immediately upon entering the produce department, I ran into a woman who knew my grandma and me well. I hadn't seen her for years, and there were very few people alive who knew us both. After greeting me with affection, without missing a beat, the woman said, "Your grandma would be very proud of you."

Stunned by her words, I choked back tears.

"Why did you say that?" I asked.

"I don't know," she said. "I just felt like you needed to hear it."

Less than ten seconds later, another woman I knew, but hadn't seen for at least a year, came into the grocery store. Spotting me and the other woman, she approached us with a huge smile on her face. More greetings, and then she said, "Have you seen the movie *Julie & Julia*?

"No," I answered. "What is it about?"

"It's about a woman named Julie who blogs about cooking Julia Child's recipes for a year. I saw it last night. It was very good."

"Did you say Julia Child?" I asked, incredulously.

"Yes." She went on to explain more about the movie, but I wasn't listening. I was too shocked to hear what she was saying. Because at that moment, I had no doubt my grandma was sending these women to me to prove she was still with me and to wish me a happy birthday.

How did I know this? Simple. My nickname for my grandma was Julia Child. I used to call her up and say, "May I please speak to Julia Child? I need a recipe." Each time my grandma would cover up her southern accent and imitate Julia Child. Then she'd share her best recipes and cooking tips. It was our running joke, and it always made me smile.

With Grandma no longer physically with me, a few tears accompanied my smile as I explained to these two women that they were both my grandma's messengers for a heavenly birthday greeting.

~ *Liza Wiemer*

SUGAR-COATED PROTECTION

*M*ichelle never participated in cemetery visits. Her mother's insistence that she adhere to an old family tradition—pregnant women did not attend funerals or visit the cemetery lest they incur the undue attention of dark forces—kept her from attending her own grandmother's funeral. Granted a reprieve once, Michelle expanded upon the old family tradition and adopted it as one of her own: she used it as an excuse to opt out of cemetery visits altogether, and she never joined her family on pilgrimages to the ancestral plot where her grandmother and other relatives were buried.

"You don't need me for the prayer service, and I know that Grandmother would not want me to be late for work because of her either," Michelle typically said as she excused herself from yearly participation in family visits to her grandmother's grave.

But when her co-worker Ruth passed away, it was expected that the entire staff in Michelle's office would attend the funeral, Michelle included. In fact, it was Michelle who was drafted to drive the group to the cemetery. Michelle fretted about going to the cemetery, but there was no way around it. Ruth had always been a dedicated worker, graciously serving coffee and tea at lunch breaks. She was the office nurturer: always the first to offer everyone assistance of all kinds, and the one to whom staff members brought their personal problems. She comforted those undergoing crises, pitched in during emergencies. There was no way that Michelle could opt out of this cemetery visit. None of the staff had known that Ruth was ill until the morning she suddenly collapsed at work. She died a week later. Shock, along with a chilling sadness, enveloped the entire staff. But for Michelle the sadness was compounded by her sheer terror of being in a cemetery. Any cemetery. A hard lump stuck in Michelle's throat the entire morning.

As she drove into the Jerusalem cemetery, Michelle could see that parking would be a major problem. Ruth had been beloved, and there were hundreds of people on their way up to Har Tamir to pay her their last respects. Finding parking was seeming hopeless when Michelle suddenly lucked out. She noticed a small curve in the road that everyone else seemed to have overlooked. Her car swerved, lurching forward and nearly hitting a low stone fence, as she braked for the spot. Michelle's passengers rushed out of the car, walking uphill to the funeral parlor, agreeing before they dispersed that as soon as the last eulogy ended they would leave quickly and assemble at the car so that Michelle could avoid heavy return traffic.

Listening to the eulogies, Michelle cried along with the crowd. Ruth was so young, not even fifty. None of her children had married yet, and Ruth would never enjoy the blessing of grandchildren. What comfort could one offer to her family? Nevertheless, as soon as the last speaker left the podium, Michelle resolutely wiped her tears and started back to the car; leaving the cemetery grounds posthaste was her foremost priority.

It was only when she returned to the car that Michelle noticed the flat tire. Her tears had dried, but she was ready to begin again. Eyes stinging, she swallowed hard, moaning. *How will I ever get out of this rut? My car looks like it's stuck here forever.*

One by one her co-workers returned to the car and stood by helpless, none of them capable of changing a tire. Michelle tossed her bag and jacket onto the front seat, determined to find help, just as the funeral procession moved slowly in her direction. Her urge was to solicit help immediately, but she couldn't dishonor the Jewish tradition of following the hearse to the freshly dug grave. There was no way she could ignore the long train of mourners on their way to Ruth's final resting place, and she motioned to her co-workers to follow her. Together they joined the long, winding mourners' procession—the car, its flat tire, and the original plan to quickly flee the cemetery temporarily forgotten.

Michelle was surprised to serendipitously find her brother in the crowd, and after the final mourner's prayer had been recited and the ritual of placing small stones on the fresh earth had been performed, she prevailed upon him to change the tire. They were walking back to the car together at a leisurely gait when suddenly Michelle started running, her brother quickly following at her heels.

"Where are you running to? What's wrong Michelle?"

"I left my car door open, my bag with my wallet, credit cards, my keys, I left my whole life on the car seat!" Michelle cried as she ran ahead of her brother.

Breathless, she reached the car, her nerves frayed from the sad day that was turning into a nightmare. *How could I have left the car door open with all my possessions inside? How could I have been so irresponsible?*

Incredibly, Michelle found her car where she had left it, the door ajar, her bag on the seat, the keys spilling out, and not a thing missing from her wallet. Everything was exactly as it had been when she abruptly joined the procession. Her brother stood there amused, his arms folded, looking at his sister's stunned face.

"Well, of course everything's intact, what do you expect? Grandmother babysat for you. Do you think she would let anyone touch or steal her granddaughter's purse or car?"

"Grandmother? Grandmother babysat my car? What are you talking about?"

"Don't you see where you're parked? You're right in front of Grandmother's grave. You don't even have to step beyond the fence. You can read the words, and see the date she died engraved on her stone."

Michelle stared at the stone facing her. She couldn't control her shock and anguish. How could it be that she had never been to her grandmother's grave? That she didn't even know where it was situated? Shame washed over her when she considered the purely accidental way she had gotten there; it was too painful to contemplate. The most sophisticated GPS device could not have guided her to the grave more efficiently. Moreover, she had an eerie feeling that it was Grandmother who had pushed her away from the car to join the mourners instead of leaving the cemetery without fulfilling her duty. So while Michelle followed the funeral procession, Grandmother had kept a vigilant eye on her belongings. Grandmother had always taken care of Michelle. She had fed her when she was hungry, read to her when she was sick, and put her to bed when she was tired, yet Michelle had never once paid her respects to a beloved grandmother who had been a source of myriad blessings to the entire family.

Humbly, Michelle stepped down to Grandmother's grave, where she read the deeply engraved, blackened letters and realized that her *yahrtzeit* (anniversary of her death) was the following evening, the second night of Chanukah. Shame at never having been to her grave persisted. How strange that Ruth had brought them together a last.

Driving home, Michelle phoned her children to let them know she was on her way.

"Hi, Mommy," said one of her little ones. "Me and Deenie walked over to Grandma's [Michelle's mother] because you didn't come home, and I forgot to take my key. Grandma gave us sugarcoated jelly doughnuts, and we helped Grandpa prepare his menorah. He said if we stay for candle lighting he'll give us Chanukah gelt, and Grandma said she would fry potato latkes for us. Please, Mommy, can we stay at Grandma's?"

The protective coat that Michelle's grandmother had once provided for her grandchildren was now in the hands of Michelle's parents. Michelle knew that the protection wasn't endless; still, she sensed it held an eternal quality.

It was as her grandmother often said, *"A mensch tracht, un G-t lacht."* Man plans and G-d laughs. No matter how we plan to manage our time, the results are divinely executed. Michelle had never meant to visit her grandmother's grave. How had she been the one person to find the prime parking spot everyone else had ignored, and how had it been that her car had suddenly ended up with a flat? Michelle suspected that it was none other than her beloved grandmother urging her to once again "come visit."

~ *Faigie Heiman*

THE CANDLELIGHT INN

Who would have thought that Dr. Wayne Dyer—one of the nation's most beloved "gurus" and popular motivational speakers, best-selling author of more than thirty books, featured speaker on PBS specials, and keynoter at conferences around the world—had had a deprived and traumatic childhood, and spent many of his early years in an orphanage?

This icon of resilience and transcendence has told his personal story many times: at various lectures, in his books, and on audiotapes. Wayne believes that "we are all connected to something bigger, a Source of some kind that moves all the pieces around in our lives,"[1] so it is not surprising that he credits part of his evolution to a mystical experience he had back in 1974, an experience that literally turned his life around 180 degrees.

In an interview on the *Bonnie Hunt Show* in 2009, Wayne recounted the eerie coincidence that led him to two things: his father's long-lost grave and his own personal redemption.

"My father walked out on our family when I was just a little boy," he told Bonnie. "My mom had three little boys—all under the age of four—when she was only twenty-two, and my father just disappeared and left. I grew up hating this man. I had so much anger towards him. He ended up marrying five additional women and he died from cirrhosis of the liver—he was an alcoholic. But for a very long time, I had no idea where he was and what had happened to him. I tried to search for him—to confront him, to ask him why he had abandoned us, and if he thought of us at all—but nobody seemed to know where he was."[2]

In 1970, Wayne experienced a bolt out of the blue. A relative of his father's suddenly called and said, "Wayne, I've heard that you have spent a lot of energy in trying to meet your father. I'm just calling to tell you that he died in 1964 in New Orleans and his body was shipped to Biloxi, Mississippi, for burial. That's all I know."[3]

Wayne's zeal to track down his dad had waned, yet his anger persisted, and he wished he had a way to confront his renegade father—even in death. But at the time that he received the phone call from his father's relative, he was in New York City teaching at St. John's University and lacked the funds to make a trek to Biloxi. However, as "luck," "chance"—or was it something else?—would have it, one of his colleagues at the university approached Wayne soon after with a request: Would he be willing to travel to Columbus, Mississippi, to review the civil rights standards being implemented at the Mississippi University for Women? Of course, he would be paid for his time and work, and his travel expenses would be covered. Now Wayne had the wherewithal to visit his father's grave in Biloxi—a mere four-hour drive from Columbus.

There was only one minor hurdle to overcome: Wayne's father's relative hadn't known in which cemetery Mr. Dyer was buried, but Wayne was not intimidated by that fact: After all, how many cemeteries could Biloxi—a small city by anyone's measure—boast?

There was exactly one car-rental place on the MUW campus, so Wayne instantly headed there when his work at the university was done. He was delighted with the car he was randomly assigned—a 1974 Dodge Coronet, practically fresh from the factory. "I notice that the Dodge had that new-car smell," Wayne remembered—and the odometer read 000.000.8 miles; it was a brand-new car delivered that very day to the college. "As I settle in behind the wheel, I reach for the seat belt and discover that it was missing. I get out of the car, take out the entire bench seat, and see the seat belt attached to the floorboard of the car with masking tape, the buckle encased in plastic wrapping and a rubber band around it. I rip off the tape and the plastic, and find a business card tucked inside the buckle. It reads: 'Candlelight Inn—Biloxi, Mississippi' with precise directions on how to get to the location. I momentarily think it's odd that this particular card is in a brand-new car and I'm actually headed to Biloxi myself."[4] But instead of simply tossing the card into a nearby wastebasket, something made Wayne put the card in his shirt pocket as he got behind the wheel.

How did a business card get stuck into the plastic wrapping that encased the seat belt in a brand-new car? How did it happen that the business card was for a place in Biloxi, Mississippi—precisely the place where the random renter of this particular car was headed? For some reason, Wayne made short shrift of the coincidence—at least then. Much later, of course, in hindsight, when he "could see clearly," he grasped that some great Source had pushed him toward his father's grave. But for now, all he could think of was his hope of finding closure, and he was single-minded in this pursuit. There was nothing that was going to deter Dr. Wayne Dyer from jumping into the car and start driving—even small mysteries that would make another man pause and reflect.

In Biloxi, Wayne stopped at a phone booth at a gas station and looked up cemeteries in the yellow pages directory hanging in the booth (remember those?) and found three listings. He started making calls. The office of the first cemetery didn't answer, and the phone at the second cemetery was busy, but the third phone call elicited a response from an elderly gentleman with a southern drawl.

"By any chance would you know if Melvin Lyle Dyer, who died ten years ago, in 1964, is buried at this cemetery?"

"Hold on," the quavering voice at the other end of the line said.

Ten minutes later, he returned. "Yes, your father is buried here.

"But," he added, "I have to tell you that this is not a 'real' cemetery. It's just a place where indigent people are frequently buried. It's on the grounds of a place called the Candlelight Inn. Problem is, it's very hard to find. It's in a very out-of-the-way location. I don't even know how to tell you how to get here by car."

Wayne pulled out the business card from his shirt pocket. On the back were precise directions to the Candlelight Inn, with arrows pointing to all the roads that would take him there— a veritable map. Wayne told the gentleman not to worry; he just so happened to know *exactly* how to get to the very obscure Candlelight Inn.

In the ramshackle hut that doubled as the cemetery's office, the elderly curator handed Wayne his father's death certificate, grimy and discolored, but still readable. Despite the anger he had carried all these years, Wayne felt a certain gratification when he read that he and his brothers were listed as "surviving sons." *He did know that he had a son named Wayne. I wonder who put this information down on his death certificate, and what he ever said to anyone about my brothers and me?* Wayne thought.

"I stayed there for three hours," Wayne told Bonnie Hunt, when he reminisced about that watershed visit. "And I did all kinds of things. I was angry at the time and stomped on his grave. And then, finally, the last few minutes that I was there, something came over me, and I said out loud to my father: 'From this moment on, I send you love. I forgive you for everything you've done.' And when I walked away from there, everything in my life had completely changed.

"When I got rid of the anger and the resentment and the hatred, my whole life totally turned around. When you carry that stuff around inside of you, it's exhausting. Mark Twain once said: 'Forgiveness is the fragrance that the violet sheds on the heel that has crushed it.' And there's a Chinese proverb that says: 'If you're going to pursue revenge, you better dig two graves, because it's going to kill you.'

"My father—the person who walked out on me when I was just an infant and who walked out on my mother and forced her to put her children into foster homes—was perhaps the most influential person in my life. Because it was through the act of forgiveness that my whole career took off. Before my visit to the cemetery, I had been overweight, drinking, in a very bad relationship, and my writing wasn't doing the things I wanted it to do. After my visit to my father's grave, I started attracting the right people into my life, lost weight, stopped drinking, and wrote *Your Erroneous Zones*, which became a bestseller fourteen days after publication."

Everything changed for Dr. Wayne Dyer after his fateful visit to his father's grave in the summer of 1974, when he extended the man who had abandoned him complete forgiveness. And a mysterious business card that miraculously found its way into a brand-new rental car that Wayne just happened to have "randomly" been assigned played no small part in his redemption, either.

~ Wayne Dyer, via various sources (see credits, page 256)

THE ENCOUNTER

One bright day, a young man was briskly walking toward his favorite café. At eighteen, he had places to go and friends to meet. This café, in the heart of Jerusalem, was the happening spot, and he had become a regular customer there—mostly of animated conversation and people watching. Suddenly, a plump little lady intercepted him on the narrow sidewalk, planting herself firmly in front of him, not allowing him to pass.

"What is your name?" she demanded incongruously, without preamble or explanation.

"My name is Loulou." He answered offhandedly, thinking she must be slightly deranged.

She shook her head, still not budging.

"No, what is your *real* name?"

"People have called me Loulou as far back as I can remember."

The stocky woman was getting annoyed. "But that is not your real name!"

"Listen, lady, I have to go somewhere."

Enforcing her stance, she wouldn't let him pass.

What does this crazy lady want from me anyway? thought Loulou. *I have never seen her before. I don't know why she chose me, of all people. Couldn't she have picked someone else? What an obnoxious person.* He looked for a way to walk around her without touching her, but he couldn't find a way to remove this human barrier without physical contact. The lady kept looking at him expectantly, as if waiting for the "right" answer to her previous question: "What is your *real* name?"

Frustrated by the young man's obvious attempts to dodge her, the strange woman became impatient. In one swooping motion she threw a handful of sand right into Loulou's face! The stinging impact caught him off guard. It took several minutes before he could finally clear the sand out of his eyes and regain his bearings. By that time, the odd lady had disappeared.

"People like that should be locked away," Loulou growled. No one else seemed to have witnessed the bizarre incident. The pedestrians nearby were hurrying to their destinations, and none stopped to offer him aid or comfort. It appeared as if they were oblivious to his discomfort and shock, as if he were the only one in the universe who knew what had just occurred. It had been a bizarre experience, and he was shaken.

Turning toward a main street and the solace of more "normal" people, Loulou was about to step off the curb when suddenly the entire neighborhood shook and rattled from the booming impact of a terrifying explosion. It came from precisely the direction toward which he had been heading. Questioning one of the frightened people rushing past him, he was told that a terrorist bomb had exploded at his favorite café. Trembling, Loulou reached the nearest phone and called his mother. After reassuring her for the fifth time that he really was OK, untouched, not even a scratch, he finally convinced his mother that he was safe and she sighed in immense relief.

"Thank God you are alive, my Loulou!"

"You know," Loulou reflected, "I would certainly be dead or wounded by now if it hadn't been for this absolutely crazy lady who barred my way. I was going directly to the café, but she just kept asking me for my real name, and she wouldn't let me pass. She even threw sand in my eyes!"

"Who was it? Didn't she tell you who she was?"

"I didn't ask. I wasn't interested in her. But because she delayed me I wasn't at the café when the bomb exploded."

"What did she look like?" his mother wanted to know.

"Well, she looked ancient . . . like she had walked out of a history book. Her eyes were very blue and penetrating."

Pried with a tumble of questions, Loulou finally gave his mother a detailed description of the woman who had barred his way. As he began to paint a fuller portrait of the woman's appearance, his mother began to shriek and cry. "Mother! Why are you crying? I am fine!"

Between tears, his mother explained: "The lady you describe as having stood in your way—deliberately delaying you—exactly matches the physical description of my own mother, your grandmother. She died when you were a baby, and I never had any pictures to show you, so there is no way you could know what she looked like. But it clearly was her. She appeared to you at that very moment to save your life!"

~ *Liliane Ritchie*

A STRANGER'S WORDS OF PRAYER

Sherry Lane shifted gears as she headed up the windy highway toward her office in the center of town. This was a familiar road, flanked by hills covered with pine trees and, as usual, crammed with cars driven by anxious commuters trying to get to work on time. Today, though, the cars were really backed up big-time—even for rush-hour traffic—and you could tell that something was different; something serious had occurred. As she slowed with the traffic, Sherry finally caught sight of the reason for the delay. A demolished car was surrounded by a crowd of well-meaning onlookers who had stopped to see if they could be of any help. Then she saw her. An unconscious woman was lying on the ground, bleeding. It was a wrenching scene. Who was she? Did she have family? Sherry began to pray heart and soul for her. She blessed her to recover wholly and fully in every way.

Months after the incident, Sherry suddenly received a telephone call out of the blue: "Are you Sherry Lane?" a female voice inquired.

"Yes, how can I help you?"

"You do not know me yet, but may I ask you a question? It is important to me."

"Why not? If I can help."

"Perhaps you remember a few months ago, you drove by the site of a car accident on the highway into town?"

"An accident?" It had been awhile, so it took Sherry some time to recall the scene. "I remember now . . . a woman was lying on the ground. My heart went out to her. But why do you ask?"

"That woman was me."

Sherry's relief was sincere "I am so glad that you are OK—thank God you are alive."

The next question, however, was even more surprising.

"May I ask you something else? When you were driving by, at that moment, did you say some prayers for me and bless me with words to recover wholly and fully in every way?"

"Yes. That's exactly what I did." Stunned by the question, Sherry had a few of her own. "I don't understand—tell me, how in the world did you know about it? How did you get my number?"

"Now I will tell you *my* story," the woman began. "I won't go into details about what happened before that horrible crash. But this is what happened afterward. I suddenly found myself floating about thirty feet above the scene of the accident, looking down, not knowing how or why I was there. I saw my crashed car and curiously watched this woman lying on the ground. It took me a while to figure out that the woman was me.

"I didn't feel any pain, just a deep, peaceful feeling. I realized I had died. I felt an invisible, but strong force drawing me upward, and I felt ready to leave, but something below me caught my attention. Brilliant sparks were floating up from one particular car that was slowly passing by my body on the ground. I noticed its license plate clearly, as if it were a street sign. These sparks were beautiful and fascinating. They had a purposeful soul quality, as if they were alive. As they took shape I realized the sparks were in reality luminescent, flaming letters! They were rising upward, twirling and dancing. I was drawn toward them, and I moved farther down to see where the letters were coming from. They were coming from the woman driving this car, and I heard the words 'full recovery and healing.' The light from these letters lifted up toward the heavens. Moments later that light came down again and embraced me with comfort and bliss. I don't remember what happened afterward.

"I regained consciousness in the hospital. The doctor told me he was amazed I survived the accident. It took me months to recover. My experience with the light was so vivid, I still remember every detail. I know it was that enfolding light that brought me back to my physical body. And remembering that light was what sped up my recovery.

"I also remembered the license-plate number of your car. That identification, together with some connections, helped me locate your telephone number. And here I am, calling to thank you for saving my life!"

Sherry was awestruck. It took her a few moments to assimilate the woman's story. "Just through a few words of prayer? I never realized how powerful that could be." It was hard to believe the story, but how else could the woman have known her license-plate number? Sherry's belief in the power of prayer was affirmed a thousandfold.

~ Liliane Ritchie

THE CONSTANT CAT

It's a cliché—a time-worn phrase we bandy around often without giving much thought to what it actually means. "Cats have nine lives," we say with a grin and a shrug, whenever a plucky feline is rescued from a treetop by a battalion of panting firemen or is run over by a car as it streaks across a road, only to miraculously pick itself up and amble the rest of the distance with aloof dignity, oblivious to the shrieks of the motorist who almost killed it, now slumped over the wheel and shaken to the core. Yes, cats *do* seem to have an uncanny way of surviving all kinds of hazards, from which they typically rebound with a bored yawn and a languorous stretch. And, truth be told, they recover from their brushes with mortality with far more grace and finesse than their human counterparts typically do.

But given the many accounts that seem to link cats in particular with intimations of reincarnation, perhaps the phrase "cats have nine lives" should be reevaluated and imbued with a new and altogether different meaning.

Lucy Mendez's story is a strong case in point. Eleven years ago, the vacant condominium on her floor in a large apartment complex was bought by a stranger, Dan Perry, who had just remarried. A widower in his thirties, Mr. Perry's beloved wife, Chrissie, had died of cancer a year before, leaving him with a brood of kids, and he was now picking up the pieces of his shattered life. He had met a woman who was divorced and also had children from her first marriage, and together they formed a blended family of eight. They needed an extra-large apartment to house all their children, so they had moved to Lucy Mendez's building to begin life anew. They were blissfully unaware of the fact that they had moved into a hornet's nest of busybodies who observed their every move very closely.

The women in the apartment complex were mostly stay-at-home wives, so they had ample time to scrutinize everyone's comings and goings. Their powers of observation were usually trained on humans only. But a strange thing happened the day that Mr. Perry and company first moved in. A sleek white cat with a brown stripe on its tail that nobody had ever seen in the vicinity of the building suddenly appeared outside the complex's front door, plunked itself down, and settled in for the night. It was cold and raining that first evening, and none of the residents had the heart to shoo it away as it curled close to the entrance for warmth. By morning it would be gone, they were sure.

The next day, however, the cat became bolder. When someone opened the front door to depart the building, the cat instantly hurtled inside, zipped up the stairs in a flash of white fur, darted up three flights, and waited in the stairwell until an innocent resident opened the exit door to descend the stairs rather than wait for the elevator. The cat flew by the surprised tenant, intent upon its final destination: the front door that led to Mr. Perry's new apartment. If we were talking about a bird or even a chicken, we could say that this is where it "alighted" or "came to roost." Since there are no comparable metaphors for cats, however, we can only less adequately say that it was at Mr. Perry's apartment that the feline put down roots, established its turf, and set up its new home. All the women in the building agreed that it was quite strange. Had Mr. Perry perchance owned the cat in his previous life? Had he abandoned it at his old home?

"No!" Mr. Perry said firmly to everyone's inquiries, insisting that he had never seen the cat before. In fact, Mr. Perry had never owned a cat, or any other animal for that matter, had never once stooped down to stroke the luxurious fur of a particularly beguiling specimen, and never felt compelled to offer neighborhood strays scraps of food or bowls of milk. He just wasn't that type of guy. No cat aficionado, he. Mr. Perry did not know where the cat had come from, or why it had chosen—out of fifty other residences in the building—to colonize *his* apartment, and his apartment only, practically from the moment he moved in. It sure was a mystery, he said, not quite as perturbed as the women of the building deemed commensurate to the situation. Although he was not an animal lover, Mr. Perry possessed a placid temperament, so when he tried to whisk the cat away from his door, it was in a gentle and mild-mannered way. Alas, the cat had a more forceful personality than its human target and was not easily deterred.

Bizarrely, like Mary's little lamb, except that it was a cat, the feline began to follow Mr. Perry everywhere he went, which "was a sight to see." But this was real life, not a beloved children's song. The cat trailed Mr. Perry all day long: to his office, to the gym, to the market, everywhere. It waited patiently outside until he reappeared: from his job, from working out, from running his errands at local stores. It simply refused to leave his side. The cat didn't shadow anyone else in the building, and it had no interest in any other member of the Perry family. It was solely on Mr. Perry that the cat focused its besotted attentions.

"Let's face it!" he threw up his hands in frustration one day. "I have a feline stalker."

And yes, the women of the building had already determined that it *was* a female cat that pursued Dan Perry so ardently, which somehow lent an extra level of significance to the mystery that was tantalizing them all.

The cat's mysterious arrival on the exact day that Mr. Perry and his family had moved in seemed more than auspicious, the women of the building agreed; it seemed *designed*. "Maybe it's Mr. Perry's first wife, making sure he's all right and being taken care of properly by his new spouse," one woman humorously suggested, never thinking that her words would be taken seriously. But the other women's eyes widened with both disbelief and clarity, and they pronounced her a genius. "Of course, that's what it is!" they exclaimed in unison. "It's his dead wife come back to watch over him." (No one said "haunt.") Soon, they started calling the cat (only among themselves, careful not to hurt Mr. Perry's feelings) "Chrissie," the name of his late, lamented wife—who was utterly faithful, they were convinced, in a way that transcended this world.

Mr. Perry, unaware of the bevy of female detectives in his building who had jubilantly solved the perplexing riddle of the cat who seemed bound to him for all eternity, had originally tried to shake off his pursuer in a variety of ways, but none had worked. People suggested that he call the pound or local humane society, but he knew the fate of strays: they were usually euthanized, and

he couldn't countenance killing any animal, let alone an innocent cat whose only crime was that she seemed to like him . . .
inordinately. He tried to lure her with food to parks that were
miles away from home, but inevitably she returned to his address.
Although the neighbors—some of whom were originally fearful
of cats—similarly caved in and also tried adopting the cat, they
were treated with icy disdain. The cat accepted their morsels tentatively, but generally shied away from everyone but Mr. Perry.
Eventually, he gave up, threw in the towel, and allowed himself to
be wooed. He ultimately became attached to the cat, feeding her
regularly, and when she had kittens, he took care of them, too.

Over time, man and cat developed a special bond, an unusual
relationship; they seemed to understand each other almost tele-
pathically. Still, Mr. Perry never recognized or acknowledged
what the neighbors had known for years: it was his first wife
who was tenaciously following him, not a lovesick cat.

This went on for eleven years. Lucy Mendez—who told
me the story—eventually moved overseas and lost contact with
Mr. Perry and the neighbors, but she never forgot the saga of
the cat that had riveted everyone's attention. Lucy knows that
the average life span of cats is twelve to fifteen years. But given
this particular cat's personality and the mission to which she's
apparently pledged, Lucy is betting that "Chrissie" isn't going to
depart our earthly realm for a long time to come.

~ *Anonymous, as told to the authors*

A MOTHER'S SIGN

Across the Atlantic from the Perrys a woman named Lindsey Cresswell, who lived in a small village in northeast England, had a strange cat encounter of her own that was witnessed by dozens of astonished onlookers. It was a very different experience from the one reported by Lucy Mendez, but in its own personal way, it too suggests there are elements of the human experience that some deem "supernatural" or "mystical," while others may simply pronounce them downright bizarre.

In 2005, Lindsey's mother—after having valiantly fought her illness for more than four years—succumbed to the cancer that had ravaged her body. Before she became too frail, Lindsey's mother would often take long, restorative walks with her daughter, during which they openly discussed the Afterlife and what they assumed happened after one passed. When her mother died at the age of sixty-nine, Lindsey—although mentally prepared for some time—was emotionally unable to let go. On the day of the funeral, she begged her deceased mother, "Please let me see you one more time, or at the very least, please send me a sign that you are OK." Lindsey's mother had always been accommodating, and Lindsey expected nothing less than pure compliance.

Still, when she first saw the ginger cat (her mother was a redhead) standing among the well-wishers crowded in front of the church as her car pulled up to the curb, she didn't view its appearance as auguring any kind of message from beyond. It was simply a stray cat that had mistakenly wandered into the throng of congregants who were waiting outside for the service to begin. Neither she—nor anyone else—gave it a second thought.

But when Lindsey entered the church and the cat dutifully followed up the steps behind her, the whispers began. Friends tried to shoo the cat out of the church, but it stubbornly stood its ground. Then it slowly ambled down the aisle, looking intently to both right and left, as if checking to see who was seated in each row. Finally, it arrived at the curtain behind which Lindsey's mother's coffin stood, dived under the curtain, and tried to leap onto the coffin but tumbled off instead. (Someone guarding the coffin related this part to Lindsey, who was unaware of this piece of the story at the time.)

"As the vicar began to chant the last prayer," Lindsey recalls, "the cat started crying at the top of its voice, mewling and caterwauling like crazy. Everyone got the goose bumps. It just wouldn't stop. The people behind the curtain tried to chase it away, and they finally got it out the back door. It had really disrupted the solemnity of the service. Rather than talking about my deceased mother, people were talking about the weird behavior of the cat instead.

"Having chased the cat out the back door, we thought we were finally done with it, but when we left the church and approached the crematorium, which was located on the same grounds, there it was, waiting for us at the front door. We tried to ignore it as we inspected the wreaths of flowers that people had sent and which adorned the small chapel, but it walked straight up to us and began to rub its back against my father's legs. Finally, my son and I both crouched down and began to stroke its fur, and its back rose up to meet our gentle hands. Strays don't usually act so friendly . . . or familiar. We didn't know *what* to make of it.

"The next day when we returned to the crematorium to pick up my mother's urn, one of the cemetery workers told us that the cat was still there, and in fact it remained there until we buried the ashes in the church's graveyard. Then the cat disappeared, never to be seen again.

"The entire episode was so strange, everyone who witnessed it was talking about it for weeks. I *did* ask my mother for a sign after she had died to let us know that she was still with us, and in retrospect, I firmly believe that this was her reply."

~ Lindsey Cresswell, as told to the authors

GRANDFATHER'S WEDDING GIFT

When my parents got divorced and my father moved away, I became a very anxious little girl, because I knew it was my father who was the breadwinner of the family, not my mom. My mother, however, immediately reverted from type; she went from being a stay-at-home wife to becoming an indomitable dynamo who held down several jobs simultaneously, making sure her only daughter was well clothed, well housed, and well fed. She was adamant that I lack for nothing. Adding to this security were my father's parents, who contributed both emotionally and financially to my care. Since they lived only several doors down from our apartment, I saw a lot of my grandparents during my youth, and they provided me with abundant love and extra "pin" money.

My mother felt exceedingly grateful to her in-laws, and when my grandmother died, she began repaying all my grandfather's kindnesses in faithful remembrance. Since he refused to hire a health aide or companion to help him, my mother began to serve ad hoc as both. She prepared his meals, ran errands for him, cleaned his home, and prepared his medicines for him, making sure each week's supply was systematically laid out in different pill boxes so there would be no chance for confusion or mistakes. She also organized his insulin syringes, and drove him to doctors' appointments and various other places where he needed to go. In short, she served as his chauffeur, nurse's aide, cook, housekeeper, and substitute daughter. She checked in on him constantly, and I did too; I always stopped to greet him after school and spent time with him so he wouldn't feel lonely. After so many years in which my grandfather helped my mother feel less alone and supported, the relationship had finally become reciprocal.

My beloved grandfather died two years before I became engaged to a wonderful young man who was an orphan. My sensitive fiancé also knew what it was like to feel bereft of a parent; he too had undergone many of the same traumatic experiences that I had. It seemed to be a match made in Heaven, with only one problem: neither of us had the money to cover even a modest wedding. I became an anxious little girl again, but my mother proceeded with the wedding plans in an almost cavalier way, booking a wedding hall, hiring a caterer, reserving a band, and ordering flowers—none of which were paid for, save the small deposit my mother put down on each. I twisted and turned at night, wondering how all this would get paid for. "Don't worry," my mother said calmly, "God will provide."

A week before my wedding, hundred-dollar bills had not yet floated down from Heaven, we had not fortuitously won any lotteries, and mysterious benefactors had not come pounding at our door. My anxiety level increased. But that very night, I had a strange dream that allayed some of my fears.

In the dream, I was sitting in my living room, which in real life was adorned with a huge chandelier on which hundreds of crystals hung. When you turned the switch on, the room would burst into light, as the crystals refracted beams of luminescence that danced on the floor and created glowing shapes. The effect was as if one had entered a pulsating disco. Since the bulbs were expensive and had to be constantly changed, my mother rarely used the chandelier, preferring the lamps scattered on the end tables instead, and she forbade me from turning it on as well. We still lived frugally. But in this dream, the chandelier was illuminated, and an unearthly radiance filled the room.

I was seated in an armchair, bedecked in my wedding gown, when my grandfather suddenly materialized in front of me, looking exactly as he had appeared before his death. He was wearing the gray button-down V-neck sweater that he had always favored, and an old-fashioned cap that was popular with the cab drivers of Montreal, where I grew up. An inveterate chain-smoker during his lifetime, my grandfather reeked of smoke, which I could smell distinctly. He held out his hand to me, and we danced, my white gown with its long train swirling on the wooden floor. Then he bent over to kiss me, and whispered that I shouldn't worry; he had money for my wedding. He handed me an envelope, and inside I found ten thousand dollars in cash. Then he disappeared, and I awoke in my bed, shaking.

I didn't tell my mother about the dream, because I didn't want to raise her expectations and give her false hope. As for me, I decided that the dream had been nothing more than just a dream: the result of either magical thinking, some stubborn faith, or the simple yearning for my grandfather's presence—all sublimated into a nocturnal fantasy.

But meanwhile time was running out, and my mother—and I—had no idea how we would pay the bills that would be due at the end of the wedding, when the caterer, bandleader, florist, and wedding hall owner would all converge for their rightful share.

One day before my wedding, my uncle, my father's brother, called my mother to tell her that, according to my grandfather's will, a certain sum of money had been put aside to pay for my wedding—if and when it should take place. Why my uncle had waited until the very last moment to tell my mother about my grandfather's provision remains a mystery to this day, and my mother was utterly stunned by this sudden turn of events, having been given no clue by my grandfather that I was named in his will. Nonetheless, we were enormously grateful to be bailed out . . . even if it was practically at the stroke of midnight.

All the anxiety that had been bottled up inside me vanished, and I approached my big night calm, relaxed, serene, and very, very happy. Not only had the tension about paying the vendors dissipated, but the fact that my grandfather had loved me so much, and made sure that I was taken care of, filled me with great joy and light, a feeling that would long endure.

The sum of money that my grandfather had left for my wedding? *Exactly* the amount that he had handed to me in my dream: ten thousand dollars. And I knew that as I danced at my wedding, twirling in my white wedding gown on the wooden floor, he was right there beside me, holding my hand.

~ *Anonymous, as told to the authors*

A SON RETURNS

On March 21, 2011, Arnold, my eighty-year-old uncle, died alone in his trailer. Arnold was a nonreligious Jew who never got to know his own heritage. Consequently, he was not familiar with the traditional Jewish belief that a human body is to be treated with reverence and buried in the ground as soon as possible after death—not cremated. So he left instructions that when he died, his body should be cremated; cremation was a much-less-expensive option than a regular burial—the fee was only six hundred dollars—and he had not been blessed with much of an estate. I was informed that his family followed his final wishes and sent his body to a crematorium.

I too had grown up Jewishly uninformed, but over time my life's path had led me back to the heritage that had been lost to my family. The opportunity I had to absorb Jewish values left me with a heightened sensitivity not only to the preciousness of the soul but to the body it leaves behind. So although I sympathized with my uncle's family I was dismayed by the cremation plans, and I set out on a mission to change their minds.

My pleas, however, did not reach their mark. My aunt and cousins felt they needed to respect Uncle Arnold's wishes, even though they too felt uncomfortable with foregoing a traditional Jewish burial. They became distraught and confused.

I decided to take action. First, I prayed countless prayers beseeching God to not let this happen. Then I contacted an organization that arranges Bible study as a merit on behalf of a departed soul. I also sent a charitable contribution to this organization to sponsor Bible study for my departed uncle, which would begin on a Tuesday, a week after he died. I later learned that on that same Tuesday night, my uncle's youngest daughter, Valerie, had a dream in which her father came to her and said, "Please don't cremate me."

Early Friday morning, I called once again to ask my cousins to do a traditional Jewish burial and not cremate their dad. Remembering Valerie's portentous dream, they finally agreed to the Jewish burial.

I called the local rabbi in Las Vegas, where the funeral was to be held, and he said that it was impossible for him to get a quorum of ten men to appear at the chapel at 1:30 in the afternoon—the time that had been arranged for the funeral, as most people are at work then. We didn't know what to do.

I flew in for the funeral, and my cousins picked me up. As we were leaving the airport, we realized we were hungry, and they agreed to join me at a kosher restaurant. In the restaurant, I told the Jewish waiter why we were in Las Vegas, and added that I was afraid that we would not have the required ten men for the prayer services. I was amazed when the waiter volunteered to gather friends to help make a quorum at the funeral!

And so, through a series of prayers, Bible study, charitable contributions, a dream, divine intervention, and the kindness of strangers, my uncle received a true Jewish burial, officiated by a respected local rabbi. All these things converged to make the funeral happen, but in my heart of hearts, I truly believe that my uncle's appearance to his daughter in the dream was the ultimate deal-breaker.

But the story doesn't end here. A few months later, my family and I decided to spend our summer vacation in Colorado (we live in Arizona, where summers are brutal), which—beyond the fantastic weather and stunning natural beauty—had the extra bonus of being the home of my three first cousins, the children of my Uncle Arnold, whom we had just buried together a few months earlier.

On the morning of our departure, just as my husband was about to load the van for our fourteen-hour trip, something made me take a pregnancy test. I was sure that my "hunch" was wrong; after all, I was forty-three, my husband was forty-six, and our youngest child was five. It didn't make sense, but something was nagging at me. I decided at the last moment that I had to find out for sure before we left; one minute later, I was staring down at a brightly colored positive result. *Oh my God!* I was in shock. I didn't know what to think. Two years earlier, I had had a miscarriage, and we thought that was the end of our child-rearing days.

I heard my kids chattering outside. "Should we get in the car now, Ma?" they called out.

"Sure, go ahead!" I called back. "I'll be right out. I just have to speak to Daddy privately, and then we'll be right on our way to Colorado!"

A few minutes later, a dazed Charlie and I climbed into the car and drove the next fourteen hours to the Rockies, contemplating our news. "It's a blessing!" Charlie had exclaimed happily. I, however, was stunned into silence. Nausea, discomfort, labor, sleepless nights. . . . How would I manage? Would everything be OK? Would our baby be OK? I was scared.

But then I calculated the due date, which turned out to be less than two weeks before the first anniversary of Uncle Arnold's death. Wow, I thought. I flashed back to just a few months earlier and the warm, loving hug my Aunt Myra had given me at her husband's funeral as she whispered into my ear, "God will repay you for your kindness." Was this it? Was our baby's soul connected in some way to Uncle Arnold? Was he somehow looking down at us right now as we made the journey to reconnect with his daughters in Colorado? I hadn't told my cousins or their mother that I was the one who had covered the expenses for their father's funeral. I had told them that a Jewish society had footed the bill; in fact, the Jewish society *had* initially laid out the money, but I was slowly paying them back. Could Uncle Arnold have pulled some strings for me in Heaven in reciprocation?

At my age, a couple weeks shy of forty-four, I was very anxious about my pregnancy. And so, when I had an ultrasound that revealed that our baby was a healthy baby boy, I cried tears of joy. In the ultrasound room, I called my three cousins. I couldn't believe it was a mere coincidence that Uncle Arnold had passed away almost exactly one year from this baby's due date. In Judaism there is a concept called "measure for measure." Our baby's soul, I believed, was very much tied to my uncle's passing. My cousins and Aunt Myra were very happy for us.

In anticipation of the delivery of our new son, I had prepared a birth plan. God, however, had his own plan.

Having done this already four times before, I envisioned an easy and speedy delivery. I would have no artificial drugs in my body, no IV, no attachments, and an amazing delivery. I would pray for my friends and family during the birth, with God's holy presence in attendance. I had everything figured out—but, of course, nothing went according to the script I had written in advance.

Eleven days after my due date, on a Wednesday evening, the baby had still not come. My OB told me that she would have to induce me the next day if the baby did not come on his own. I was entering my forty-second week of pregnancy. Being induced was not part of my birth plan, and I was very upset.

At 7:40 the next evening, the hospital called, telling me it was time to come in. An hour later, under a very full, low moon, we arrived at the hospital, but I was not in labor, so checking in felt somewhat surreal.

Soon after we checked in, the nurse came in to examine me. Their new birth plan was to begin the inducement process, then allow me to go to sleep, and I would wake up Friday morning in labor. The baby, however, had no more interest in this plan than he'd had in mine. By the time the nurses were ready to induce, he had already taken the initiative to get things moving on his own—I started getting contractions. There went the sleep idea.

The labor was very hard and long. Finally at 2:07 p.m., our beautiful little son was born—exactly a year to the very day of Uncle Arnold's passing. Mazel tov!

From the start, it was clear to all of us that we would name our son for Uncle Arnold. However, no one could figure out what his Hebrew name had been—or if he had even been given one to begin with. There was no question that we wanted to honor Uncle Arnold's memory, so we chose an *A* name for our son—Azriel, which means "My help is God." Since my husband and I began this journey of returning to our roots, we have felt that God has always been helping us along, every step of the way. Ultimately, we wanted to thank God for bestowing on us this son of our old age, and also give a special nod to Uncle Arnold . . . who clearly had a hand in the proceedings, too.

~ *Robin Davina Meyerson*

INVITATIONS TO A WEDDING

*G*randmothers are such sticklers for details.

You would think that if they were to undertake the very long journey from the Afterlife to this one, it would have to be for an excellent reason. Wars, famine, fires, ill health, apocalypses . . . those were the usual reasons they descended to earth—wasn't it?—to warn their loved ones to flee, to extinguish the blaze, to get out of the house quick, to take better care of themselves, to *eat*, for God's sake! Something like that, right? Wrong! At least in Karen Jordan's case, there was no earth-shattering reason for her beloved grandmother to appear to her in a dream. At least not from her perspective. But Karen's grandmother was a stickler for details, and clearly Karen was not.

The incident happened many decades ago, but it was so vivid, so real, and, in its own quiet way, so awesome that Karen has never forgotten it. She was getting married in May 1979, and one month beforehand was in the midst of a flurry of last-minute arrangements, including getting out the wedding invitations that she had delayed mailing for far too long. Karen stayed up late one night addressing the envelopes and inserting the invitations inside. When she was finished collating them, she sealed the envelopes and went to sleep, sighing with relief, sure she was done. But her beloved grandmother, Bubbe Devorah Leah, who had died several years before and clearly scrutinized everything Karen did on this earthly plane, did not agree. She came to Karen in a dream that night to give her a little nudge.

In the dream, her grandmother was studying the wedding invitation very closely, looking at every word, and then she asked Karen, in her signature singsong Yiddish accent: "Forest Park Jewish Center? Where *is* Forest Park Jewish Center?"

Karen woke up from the dream sorely disappointed. If her *bubbe* had come all the way from the Other World, couldn't she at least have wished me her mazel tov, poured other blessings on her head, or given her some marital advice? Instead, all she wanted to know was where Forest Park Jewish Center was located? What kind of dream was that? It was a strange question to ask. Did it have any significance whatsoever?

Karen stared at the sealed envelopes piled up in the boxes, ready to be mailed, and then suddenly clapped her hand to her forehead in self-castigation. "Idiot!" she murmured to herself. "You forgot to include the little card with the directions to the hall!" The caterer had provided the cards, which are standard, but Karen had failed to insert them into the invitation package.

She opened all the envelopes, inserted the little cards with the directions, and sealed them again.

Lucky thing her *bubbe* made her fortuitous appearance before Karen had dropped them at the post office!

~ *Karen M. Jordan, as told to the authors*

TESTIMONY

*L*ong before *Schindler's List* inspired Steven Spielberg to embark upon a massive project to videotape the testimony of Holocaust survivors for posterity, an American Holocaust historian had begun a similar, albeit much smaller, initiative of her own. Survivors streamed to the crumbling offices where she worked, having been alerted through the grapevine that the historian was seeking "witnesses." Since the bulk of this work took place in the mid-1980s—some four decades after the end of World War II—most of the people the historian filmed were middle-aged and older. Consequently, she was startled one day when a young woman—barely out of her teens—arrived at her office and announced that she had come to "give testimony."

"You won't believe this," the receptionist said when she knocked on her superior's office door.

"What's the matter?" the historian asked.

"There's a young girl in the reception area, saying she's come to give testimony. As a Holocaust survivor."

The historian confronted the girl in the waiting room. "Is this some kind of prank or joke?"

"Look, I know it sounds implausible," the girl said, "but every night I have terrible nightmares about being in the Holocaust. Everything is so vivid, so real. I have these flashbacks that feel so authentic. My nights are torture, I cannot get any rest, and I thought if I came to you, I might exorcise these demons that haunt me all the time. Please, can you take my testimony?"

"Are you Jewish?"

"No, I'm Italian Catholic."

"Do you live in a Jewish neighborhood?"

"No, I live in a very Italian neighborhood."

"Well, do you have any Jewish friends? Classmates? Have you taken any Jewish studies courses in college?"

"No, no, and no," the girl answered.

"Well, have you read any Holocaust literature or seen any Holocaust movies?" the historian continued, trying to find a rational reason that would explain the girl's nightmares.

"No, I haven't. "

"How old are you?"

"Twenty."

"This all doesn't make any sense," the historian said, skeptical and at the same time intrigued, "but come into the room, and I'll videotape you anyway." She believed that this girl was trying to perpetrate a hoax, but to what end the academician couldn't fathom. Nonetheless, the scholar was naturally inquisitive, and she was curious to hear what the girl had to say.

For someone who insisted that she had never read a book about the Holocaust nor taken any kind of course, the girl turned out to be extremely knowledgeable about the circumstances leading up to the war. More surprisingly, she didn't say that she had been imprisoned at Auschwitz or Buchenwald or Majdanek, the "famous" camps about which much information had already been disseminated. Rather, she said, she had been confined to a small, obscure women's camp that very few people had ever heard of. The testimony—with very detailed descriptions of life at the camp, including specifics about the personalities interned there, the conflicts among bunkmates that sometimes erupted, and the friendships that were often forged—took hours.

"I know a few people who survived this camp," the historian told the girl when it was over. "I'm going to ask them to view your video."

She waited for them to debunk the girl's testimony, but instead the survivors of the camp were astounded. "How did she know *this*? How did she know that? No one knew about this woman's abortion. . . . How could she know about that altercation? No one ever wrote about it!" Everyone who viewed the testimony swore that every single detail was authentic. From whom and how could the girl have obtained this information?

"I was astounded myself," the historian told me many years ago, when I personally asked her about "oddball theories" about the reincarnation of Holocaust victims. As a lark, I had recently gone to a past-lives regression session with a renowned hypnotist; I regressed to a past life where I was a woman incarcerated in Sobibór, the infamous death camp—I even learned my former name during the regression. When I tentatively called the historian to ask if there were any records of Sobibór inmates, she told me instead of the young girl's story.

"So why didn't you alert the press, tell someone?" I pressed. "The story is amazing!"

"You're right," she agreed. "But had I come forward with the story, I would no longer be regarded as a scholar, only a quack. My credibility would have been utterly ruined."

That is why I am being purposefully vague and keeping the historian's identity anonymous. However, I never forgot her story, and twenty-five years after I first heard it, I still feel a deep sense of mystery whenever I recall it.

And yes, the scholar did tell me that there was a book that contained the names of the Sobibór inmates, but all these years I've been too frightened to consult it. Frightened of being disappointed? Not quite. Simply too frightened to confront a dimension that few of us understand or can ever hope to penetrate in our lifetimes. What would I do if the name that came to me during the past-lives session was actually inked in the Sobibór book? More than wonderment, it would summon up a certain sense of terror and open up portals to enigmas beckoning with possibilities that I just don't know if I want to explore.

But my experience did elicit the scholar's own tale, and I have carried it in my heart as a heavy responsibility for years.

Would she want to share it—after all this time? Or would she want to die with the secret she apparently only told me?

Since she was an academic, beholden to the truth, my sense is that at this late stage of her life she would want other people to know, which is why I am recounting it today.

~ *Yitta Halberstam*

THE RIGHT TIME

Steve and I got married in March 1998. Just a few months later, I was pregnant with our first child. I was overjoyed and excited, as was our entire family. My first appointment with the obstetrician was scheduled for when I would be eight weeks pregnant. But before that appointment, I had a visitation from my deceased grandfather, Jerry, who came to me in a dream.

In the dream, he appeared by my bed and said, "Erin, you have a blighted ovum. You're going to have a miscarriage. But don't worry; things will work out for the best." He then showed me an image of a little baby girl being passed around from one family member to the next at Thanksgiving. I woke instantly, in a panic. What the heck is a blighted ovum? I asked myself. I had another pregnancy test in my possession and I took it immediately. Still pregnant. I chalked up the dream to bad Chinese food and went on about my day, happily pregnant.

Two weeks later, Steve and I went to the doctor's appointment. She decided to do an ultrasound to date the pregnancy and see if she could detect the heartbeat. During the ultrasound the doctor said, "Hmm, I don't think you're as far along as you think you are. I see the sac, but I'm not really seeing the baby. Are you sure you are not actually just five and a half weeks along instead of eight?"

I told her I was very sure of my dates. Remembering what my grandpa said, I asked, "Could it be a blighted ovum?"

The doctor looked at me and said, "Wow, how do you even know that word? We haven't used that term since the fifties. Nowadays we call it a molar pregnancy or a missed pregnancy. We'll just do a couple of blood tests to make sure your HCG levels are going up instead of down."

I told her about the "dream" I had of my grandfather, during which she looked at me like I was slightly crazy.

I took the blood tests. I got the results. My doctor called me, and the first thing she said was, "Does your grandfather give out lottery numbers? You do indeed have a blighted ovum. I'm so sorry; you're going to have a miscarriage."

A blighted ovum, for those of you not in the know, happens when a fertilized egg attaches itself to the uterine wall, but the embryo does not develop. Cells develop to form the pregnancy sac, but not the embryo itself. A blighted ovum usually occurs within the first trimester before a woman knows she is pregnant. It's really the only way you can be "sorta pregnant." You are pregnant enough to register on a pregnancy test, but there is no baby.

The doctor asked if I wanted a D&C or if I wanted to simply let nature take its course and eventually I would naturally miscarry. We took the second option. In a few weeks, I did have the miscarriage. I wasn't upset by the experience because I had been forewarned by my grandfather that it was going to happen. I truly felt that the little soul who had originally decided to incarnate with us had decided to wait. We were going through a tough time financially, and to be honest, we weren't ready for a baby. It was a blessing in disguise.

A year later, we got pregnant again, and I gave birth to our first daughter, Emily. This time everything was right. I remember showing off our daughter to all our relatives at Thanksgiving. I could practically feel Grandpa smiling down at us. He turned out to be right, about everything.

~ *Erin Pavlina*

LAST WORDS

All his life, Andy Golembiewski was known as both a mischievous prankster and a warmhearted Good Samaritan. As the owner of a tavern in a small town in Pennsylvania, he was a neighborhood fixture with a reputation for playing pranks on his customers but also for lending them money when they were short. He believed that helping another human being in time of need was the greatest good a man could do.

He provided well for his family members in life and, they believe, worked in mysterious ways to provide well for them after he died, too.

At the age of eighty-three, Andy contracted prostate cancer, and in the summer of 1997 his condition took a noticeable turn for the worse. One night in August, he fell into a coma, and his grieving family gathered at his bedside, braced for the inevitable. When hope for an improvement in Andy's condition had all but vanished and he had been unconscious for hours, his eyelids suddenly fluttered. His fingers began to quiver, and his body trembled. Then his eyes flew open, and they darted around the room with a gleam of intelligence and lucidity. He propped himself up on his arms, looked his granddaughter in the eye, and said loudly and clearly: "1 . . . 6 . . . 9 . . . 5." And then, as suddenly as he had stirred, he fell back onto the bed, unconscious, and a few hours later he died.

His relatives didn't know what to make of it. They all agreed that Andy had appeared perfectly rational and clear-headed when he had uttered the four numbers. But what did these numbers mean?

They had clung to the hope that he would awaken from the coma to bask in their love and receive a last embrace. They had yearned for some final words of love from Andy, or some crowning and climactic nugget of wisdom that would cap his life and serve as a departing testament. But . . . numbers? What kind of message from the grave was that?

"Those were the very last words he uttered," recounted his daughter-in-law. "Nobody could figure out the significance of this particular sequence of numbers. It wasn't anybody's birthday, phone number, address, anything. Nothing connected."

For the next several hours, the relatives experienced a seesaw of varying emotions: grief over Andy's death, puzzlement over his last words. They could not shake their conviction that Andy's recitation of the numbers held import, and they tried to make sense of his near-death communication. What could those numbers mean?

It was Andy's son, Tony, who finally suggested that they play the Big Four Lottery, which was being held the next day.

The next evening, they celebrated a very bizarre and bittersweet lottery win of $23,500.

"Andy!" his widow screamed, as the numbers were called up. "You're so concerned about your family, you even paid for your own funeral!"

The win was ironic, Andy's grandson, reflects. "During his lifetime Andy was opposed to gambling and had never even once played the lottery. When he went on family vacations to resorts where there were casinos, he tagged along in order to ogle the women, not to play the slots!"

"He was a prankster," said his granddaughter. "I think he's up there laughing that we only put a dollar on the number." (Too bad they didn't take him more seriously.)

"He was so kindhearted," another relative said, "that he felt compelled to look out for his family—even after he was gone."

~ *Yitta Halberstam*

SAYING GOOD-BYE

t wasn't the screeching of feral cats coming from the backyard; it wasn't the squealing of car tires rounding a bend too fast; it wasn't the howling wind rattling the garbage cans outside. There was no way she could possibly describe the unearthly noise that woke her from a deep sleep one night in 1978, but the terrible keening instantly ejected Winnie Alley from her bed and onto the rug near her bed.

"I don't remember leaping out of my bed," she says. "It just happened. I simply found myself standing on the rug, trembling with shock."

As she sat back on the edge of her bed, shivering in the darkness, Winnie suddenly noticed a bright light bouncing off the wall she faced. Within the light flickered a strange pattern or screen, a maze of what could have been a series of coat hangers, arranged in a specific design. "Then I became aware that my old friend Sam, dressed in his full Canadian air force uniform, was standing in my bedroom doorway, not four feet from me," Winnie recalls.

Winnie didn't dwell on Sam's strange behavior or his incongruous visit. Why a casual friend whom she hadn't seen for a long time would invade her home at such a late and inappropriate hour, and why his entrance had been preceded by a bizarre sound-and-light show, were issues that didn't seem to unsettle her much. Winnie got mad instead.

"I began to rail at him angrily," she remembers. "*What was he doing in my bedroom!* is all I wanted to know. My parents were downstairs, hadn't he seen them? More important, hadn't they seen him? What did he say to them? What did they say to him? How could they have allowed him to come upstairs and enter my room?

"As I continued berating him, Sam's image slowly began to recede. He said nothing. As I watched, Sam continued to fade until he vanished into the walls of the house. He was gone.

"I immediately regretted my sharp tongue. I had given Sam no chance to speak or explain. I wanted him to return, but the experience was over. The room had reverted back to its normal shape. Both the unworldly yowling which had roused me from sleep and the unusual light which had cast its beams on my walls had evaporated, along with Sam. The only thing for me to do was to return to my bed."

Winnie had met Sam in 1971, when both worked at a military base in Montreal. At work, they often stopped near their desks or in the hallways to converse, sometimes just engaging in idle chitchat, at other times exchanging personal views on serious subjects. Many of their discussions had been stimulating and meaningful, and had left their mark. Why had she let the threads of their friendship loosen?

Eventually, Winnie had returned to her home in Nova Scotia, and Sam went out West to Alberta. "We lost touch, but I still remembered the ideas we had discussed and the stories we had told one another, some of which had left quite a deep impression," Winnie said. "I wondered what was happening in his life, and why he had appeared to me as a vision, because that's what I was convinced had occurred that fateful night. I didn't think it was a dream. It seemed more real than that."

A few weeks after her uncanny nocturnal experience, Winnie decided to visit her old workplace, where she had first met Sam. "I needed to know what was going on. I figured that someone had to be left from the old crew, someone who would know where he was. I took the train to Montreal, and as I disembarked at the station, I noticed that it seemed unusually quiet and empty. As I walked across the terminal, I was shocked to see a familiar figure striding briskly from the opposite end of the hall in my precise direction—a person who had been both my friend and Sam's. In retrospect, it seemed destined that we meet. After expressing our mutual amazement at the divine fate that made our paths intersect, we decided to go for coffee.

"As we sat down at the counter, my friend turned to me with a grave face and asked: 'Do you know about Sam?' 'What?' I tensed. 'He committed suicide.' 'No! Where? When? Why?' My friend recounted all the terrible details while my heart tore into little shreds. I wanted to unburden myself and share what had happened that night with Sam, but I was unable to confide in my friend. I was so ashamed. My intense regret at how I had treated Sam returned, washed over me in waves, and became deeper and deeper. Later, I aimlessly walked the streets of Montreal for the remainder of the day. The face of every man who walked toward me became Sam's face. It took some time for me to recover.

"According to my friend, Sam's death occurred just before his birthday. His visit to me apparently took place at the same time. Meeting our mutual friend in the railway station was equally unexpected and improbable, although that meeting did occur in the real physical world, while my meeting with Sam obviously did not. To this day, some thirty-six years later, I still sense that he is near. I often wonder if he knows how much I have regretted banishing him in such a rude manner when he chose to visit me and say good-bye."

~ *Winnie Alley*

SIMULPATHITY

*T*oday we all accept as fact the concept that concrete information can be digitally transmitted via such devices as computers, GPS systems, and smartphones—technology that would have astounded previous generations—but most of us have a far more difficult time believing that emotional information can be conveyed psychically or spiritually through means we don't really understand either. There are certainly far more people who take for granted the reality of a videochat between someone in Japan and someone in the United States than who accept the notion of a telepathic connection linking two individuals from those same countries.

Dr. Bernard Beitman, a respected psychiatrist who is the former chair of the Department of Psychiatry at the University of Missouri-Columbia and who has received two national awards for his psychotherapy training program, is currently at work on a major book about synchronicity. He is planning to create a new transdisciplinary field of "coincidence studies," having already conceptualized categories of different types of coincidences that are part of the human experience.

Dr. Beitman's fascination with coincidence comes from his own individual encounters with a series of such events during the course of his lifetime. One of the categories that Dr. Beitman breaks down into a subclass of coincidence is *simulpathity—* the simultaneous experience by one person of another person's distress at a distance." Dr. Beitman's coinage of this term was inspired by a personal and traumatic experience that he underwent more than four decades ago. The event occurred in 1973, but it had such a major impact on him that he remembers it as vividly today as when it first occurred—first, because of the emotional nature of the event, and second, because it helped catalyze his fascination with and eventual study of synchronicity.

Dr. Beitman was a young medical resident at the time, living in a stately Victorian home in San Francisco, far from his original roots in the East. At 11:00 p.m. on February 26, 1973, Dr. Beitman was standing in his kitchen when he suddenly began choking, out of the blue. "It was as if something was stuck in my throat and just wouldn't come out," he remembers, "but the strange thing was, I hadn't eaten anything. Yet, all of a sudden I was choking, not able to stop, and feeling as if I would die if I couldn't get the foreign object out of my throat. But nothing was inside, nothing at all. Nonetheless, I couldn't stop, and I felt as if I were being asphyxiated. It took a long while until the spasms ended, and the whole experience was quite terrifying.

"The next morning, I learned that in Wilmington, Delaware, at 2:00 a.m., which was 11:00 p.m. San Francisco time, the exact time that I had been choking, my father had been choking on his own blood in his throat and had died."

How could this have happened? Dr. Beitman chalks it up to simulpathity, and over the duration of his career, he has gathered myriad reports of similar cases—especially ones concerning identical and extroverted twins. "Parents too have also experienced this phenomenon with their children," Dr. Beitman adds.

One of the oldest stories on record, which Dr. Breitman unearthed during his research, occurred in 1863 in England; it is documented in the book *Phantasms of the Living*, by E. Gurney, F.W.H. Myers, and F. Podmore, published in 1886. "A young man had been attending a party with close friends, and the evening had been extremely enjoyable for him. Just before midnight, the hostess asked him to play the piano—a skill at which he was quite adept. . . . As his fingers nimbly flew over the piano keys, he suddenly became overcome by an indescribable feeling. For no apparent reason, he became intensely sad . . . and was led away from the piano in hysterics. The next morning, the young man received a telegram from his sister reporting that his father had died that night . . . at exactly fifteen minutes before midnight." Dr. Breitman has gathered hundreds of such stories, all of which bear witness to the validity of his newly coined term.

"The realization that I was choking at the exact same time that my father was choking led me to a much more open sensitivity to these kinds of stories," he reflects. "People can and do feel the pain of those people with whom they feel close, even if they are at quite a distance away from them."

These connections transcend both time and space, and "although we just don't know what it is exactly," according to Dr. Beitman, "they do in fact occur."

~ *Bernard Beitman, MD, as told to the authors*

THE PURPLE ARROW

In the fall of 1990, through the marvelous matchmaking of my friend, Tina, I met Neil Bishop, whom I recognized as my beloved, and we wed in October 1992.

When Neil was three years old, his parents—Barbara and Jerome Sheftel—divorced. His mother remarried, and Neil was raised mainly by his mother and stepfather.

Jerome (or Jerry, as he was more commonly called), was born in 1929, and he served in the American occupation army in Japan after World War II. He lived alone and was working as a salesman in a bedding store when I first met him. About seven months after Neil and I were married, we received a call from the coroner's office. Jerry had taken his life, after suffering what seemed to be a debilitating stroke. Naturally, this was shocking news. And while Neil and I had compassion for Jerry's decision not to carry on under conditions he deemed unlivable, we were troubled by his suicide. We were concerned about whether he would be able to find some form of peace in the Afterworld.

Neil was working at the time in the used-book annex of L.A.'s erstwhile metaphysical bookstore the Bodhi Tree. After Neil's bereavement leave ended, I went by the store one day to visit him and was drawn to a book called *Angel Letters*, accounts of angelic intervention submitted to author Sophy Burnham by readers of her earlier work, *A Book of Angels*, which I had also read and enjoyed.

I bought *Angel Letters* and loved the stories so much that I purchased two more copies and sent them to friends. I then came across something that caught my eye in the used hardcover that I had originally bought for myself, something that made me do a double take and peer at the book more closely.

On page 117, midway down the page, a thin purple arrow had been carefully drawn around a single word: *Jerome*. The arrow pointed to a line on the facing page, which read: "but not to fear, that it would never be too bad for me." This arrow, the one and only mark in the entire 140-page book, served as a mysteriously reassuring message to Neil and me.

Jerry Sheftel's ashes are buried in Los Angeles National Cemetery, established for the burials of war veterans, and though he never received a Purple Heart, Jerome was indeed graced with a Purple Arrow.

~ *Cindy Lubar Bishop*

MY GRANDMA, THE ANGEL

I boarded the flight in Los Angeles with tremendous trepidation about what I would find on the other end in Israel. My daughter was pregnant and about to give birth to her first child, and my first grandchild! So much nervous anxiety and anticipation filled me, I could barely find my way to my seat. My joy was only slightly dampened by some complications that my daughter was having with the pregnancy, but I tried not to focus on that and think only good thoughts. I argued with myself that lots of first-time mothers have complications, but things always turned out for the good, right? Somehow I was having trouble convincing myself of this as I made this long flight alone to be at my daughter's side, no matter what might happen. I desperately wished I had company to calm me down, instead of having to wing it solo.

As I reached my assigned seat, I was completely taken aback when I discovered that it was the middle one, between two ultra-Orthodox men! How was that going to even be possible for fifteen hours? Even though I wasn't a religious Jew myself (at least not then), I knew how ill at ease both men would be with a female tucked between them! (In Orthodox Judaism there are strict religious laws prohibiting any kind of physical contact between men and women who are not immediate family members.) I tried not to think about how I would be able to keep my head propped up straight while I was asleep, or how I could avoid accidentally leaning over to either side while my body was in repose. This was going to be very tricky.

I'm a pretty outgoing and happy person, so I thought that the best way to approach the situation was to confront it head-on and immediately try to break the ice. The man on my right had his head buried inside a Jewish holy book, his long black coat tucked into the sides of his chair, his long *payot* (side curls) bobbing gently as he swayed ever so slightly over the text. Oy! There may as well have been a curtain stretched between us since I could see that there was not going to be any eye contact here whatsoever. OK, I told myself, I understand. Then I looked to my left. This man also had on his long black coat, payot tucked around his ears, and Jewish text on his lap; it seemed as if I was sitting between two religious bookends.

I was feeling very out of place and uncomfortable about the whole situation myself. I didn't want to cause them distress, and the whole thing was awkward. Just as I was about to try to catch the flight attendant's attention and ask for a seat change, the second man turned toward me, smiled, and said, "Good morning!" All right, I thought, this might have some potential. You see, at the time I was around three years away from becoming a returnee to Orthodox Judaism (*baal teshuva*), so my dyed red hair, my cute pair of comfy sweatpants, and my lower-neckline-than-I-wished-I'd-worn shirt made me feel like I wasn't either of these men's dream seat partner on a transatlantic flight!

I replied hello back and told the man my name, and politely inquired about his. He told me that his name was Rabbi Meir

Feldman (I've changed the name to protect his privacy). I told him that our family knew a rabbi whose name was Shlomo Feldman, and did he happen to know him? He said that, yes, it was his father. I verified with him where his father's synagogue was located in Los Angeles, and he confirmed that in fact we were talking about the one and the same rabbi! (Since Los Angeles has close to three-quarters of a million Jews, this was pretty astounding.)

I told Rabbi Feldman that we had not been in touch with his father since 1975, when I was getting married in Israel and needed a letter to present to the *beit din* (rabbinical court) in Israel proving that I was in fact Jewish. As this little interaction began to get more interesting, he asked me how I had originally come into contact with his father. (Perhaps he couldn't help notice my clothing choice for the long flight and wondered about the existence of heretofore unknown nonreligious relatives on his father's side of the family?)

I told him that my grandmother had sponsored the rabbi and his entire family to come to the United States after World War II had ended. Although she couldn't personally afford the expense, she had nonetheless gone to different homes in Los Angeles—door to door—asking for donations. She had held backyard fund-raising luncheons, charging her friends and neighbors a fee to partake of her delicious meals, and generally did whatever she could to scrape together the money to help this family. I asked him, did he know my grandmother? I told him that her name was Rose Fleischman.

He straightened up in his chair, and responded with a

warm smile, "Your grandmother was Rose Fleischman? Rose Fleischman was an angel!"

I was absolutely stunned that he had responded in such a warm and excited way. He went on to tell me that she had done so much for their family that none of them would ever forget her name. As I sat and listened, tears began to well up in my eyes. How could it be that only because of such a seemingly random seat assignment I was sitting next to a man who had known my grandma? It appeared practically impossible. (I wasn't yet familiar with the religious Jewish concept of *Hashgacha Pratis*—divine providence.) I began to feel a sense of well-being envelop me. My anxiety about the seating arrangements dissipated, as did the overwhelming fear about my daughter's upcoming delivery, which had threatened to consume me during the entire trip. I had a strong feeling that my grandmother, whom I had not seen since I was eight years old, was actually sitting beside me in the seat.

As I sat contemplating the extraordinary coincidence that had just unfolded, I was slightly disappointed when the eagle-eyed flight attendant—who apparently had noticed my initial discomfort at being seated between two religious men—informed me that she had arranged for me to sit in another row next to a woman. I said good-bye and safe travels to Rabbi Feldman and settled into my new seat. I felt Grandma relocate along with me. She was still sitting beside me, I was sure, reassuring me that all would be well. I believed her.

My granddaughter, Emuna Sarah, was born by C-section, and she was absolutely healthy, as was my daughter. By the time the delivery took place, my tension was completely gone; after my experience on the flight with Rabbi Feldman and my Grandma, I was positive that everything would work out fine, exactly as it did. And as a sweet side note—and something I realized only recently—my daughter and her husband threw a wonderful party for their new daughter five weeks later, which just happened to be the exact date of Grandma Rose's *yahrtzeit* (anniversary of her death).

~ *Cena Gross-Abergel, granddaughter of Rose Fleischman*

THE WILL

$\mathcal{M}$any "dream" stories about deceased relatives can truly produce serious reverberations in the lives of the people to whom they occur—changing their destinies in both large and small ways, even saving them from certain death—but few actually end up being chronicled in legal documents and law textbooks. Yet that is precisely what happened when a dream catalyzed an unusual and famous dispute in legal history, *Chaffin v. Chaffin*, a conundrum of a case that was brought to court in North Carolina in 1925, although it was settled before the trial really got under way.

In 1905, farmer James L. Chaffin of Mocksville, North Carolina, made his will, which stipulated that upon his death his entire estate was to pass to his son, Marshall Chaffin. While newcomers to the story might view James's bequest as exceedingly generous, that would be the case only if they were unaware of the fact that four other principal members of the family were totally disregarded and completely left out, namely Chaffin's wife and his three other sons, John, James, and Abner.

Insofar as the historians who recorded the case for posterity were concerned, there was no known animus between the various family members; everyone seemingly lived in harmony and peace. James Sr. had a good relationship with each and every one of his sons and his wife, and his family members were mystified—not to mention stunned—that he chose to omit them from his will. Later, some neighbors would claim that James Sr. had always seemed to favor Marshall, while others whispered that it was Marshall's imposing wife, Susie, who had convinced her father-in-law to leave everything to her husband.

The scandalous omission set tongues wagging, and rumor-mongers worked overtime. But no one ever really knew what lay at the bottom of it. The facts were that the will left everything to Marshall—designated him executor, too—and disinherited everyone else.

In September 1921, James Sr. died and his demise too sparked gossip. Some neighbors (and, later, historians again) said it was a heart attack that did him in, while others maintained it was the injuries he had sustained as the result of a severe fall a few months earlier that brought him to the doorstep of the Grim Reaper. However, it was not so much the cause of his death that was so critical, but rather its consequences. Marshall obtained probate on the will relatively fast—just a few weeks after his father's death—leaving his bereaved mother and three brothers shocked, destitute, and uncannily silent. Were they submissive, beaten down, defeated? No one knows why, but they did not contest the will, bowing to James's wishes in martyred resignation, and sadly, Marshall made no effort whatsoever to compensate any of them—including his own mother—for their loss.

Marshall, however, didn't end up being around long enough to enjoy the fruits of his father's labor: he died only one year after his dad, and now the property was left in the hands of his wife and their only son.

But in Heaven (or was it Hell?), James Sr. apparently did not enjoy the rest of the weary or the dead. Those of us who are fanciful can well imagine that, in hindsight, from the vantage point of time and space, James Sr. realized that he had committed a grave injustice in disinheriting his family members. Legal redress had to be served. But how could he instigate change from the very inconvenient place where he was now situated?

Four years after his death, James Sr. launched his plan. He began making frequent appearances in the dreams of his second son, James Pinkney Chaffin, in the summer of 1925. In the dreams James Sr. would stand with a mournful expression at his son's bedside, remaining uncharacteristically silent (he had apparently been quite the chatterbox when he was alive). The visitations continued in the exact same manner for several weeks, until one night the dream changed. This time James Sr. came to his son's bed dressed in an old black overcoat, a garment that he had not worn during previous visits. But James Pinkney recognized it right away: it was his father's own overcoat, which was frayed from years of use. James Sr. opened the front of the coat and spoke to his son for the first time: "You will find something about my last will in my overcoat pocket." Then the visage of his father evaporated, and James Jr. was left shaking, rubbing his eyes and wondering if he had hallucinated the whole thing.

But when he woke up the next morning, James was convinced that what had transpired the previous night was much more than a mere dream—it was a message, a directive, a clarion call for action. *My father was trying to tell me that there is a second will somewhere—and it has the power to overturn the one that left everything to Marshall and his family!* Energized by the revelation, James Pinkney sprang out of bed before dawn's first light and headed to his mother's home nearby to hunt for the old coat. Alas, it was not there, having been given by his mother to her oldest son, John, who had moved to a farm a county away. Never had twenty miles been traversed so fast! James Pinkney was pounding on his brother's door long before the cows were milked or the chickens' eggs collected for the day. He excitedly recounted his dream of the previous night, and together the brothers ransacked the farmhouse for the missing coat until it was successfully unearthed.

At first, a superficial examination of the coat yielded no clues. John began to cast skeptical looks in his brother's direction, as if to say, *A dream* made you wake me up? But James was a man possessed. He was certain that the dream meant something, so he continued to inspect the coat closely, rubbing his hands over every inch of the fabric, outside and in. That's when he realized that the inner lining of the coat had been cut and restitched. Sure enough, inside the lining was a piece of paper, rolled up and tied with string.

It wasn't a will they found, though, or any other kind of document either. Just a tattered slip of a note with a few words scribbled on it: "Read the 27th chapter of Genesis in my daddy's old Bible." What was significant, however, was the fact that the note bore James Sr.'s unmistakable imprint: his distinctive scrawl, his unique script, quite simply the way everyone remembered he signed his name.

James Jr. was jubilant with their find, but circumspect, too. On his return trip to his mother's home (where he rightly assumed that his grandfather's old Bible could be found), he stopped to pick up Thomas Blackwelder, a neighbor and close friend, renowned for his integrity, and asked him to accompany him. James felt that he was on the threshold of something momentous and might need a respected member of the community to witness whatever would occur. Blackwelder readily agreed.

Initially, James encountered frustration and despair when his mother said that while she vividly remembered the Bible of which he spoke, she had totally forgotten where she had placed it after his father's death. James, Blackwelder, and Mrs. Chaffin exhaustively searched her house, room by room, rummaging through closets, cupboards, cabinets, and drawers, the drama and the stakes at hand reaching a high nervous pitch even as the place was turned upside down. Finally, at the bottom of an old chest in an upstairs room, the Bible—somewhat rotted and in pieces—was discovered.

James and Mrs. Chaffin watched carefully as Thomas Blackwelder turned the pages to Genesis 27, where he found two pages folded to form a pocket. He slowly drew out of that pocket a piece of paper, on which the following words were written—in James Chaffin's recognizable and verifiable handwriting:

After reading the 27th chapter of Genesis, I, James L. Chaffin, do make my last will and testament, and here it is. I want, after giving my body a decent burial, my little property to be equally divided between my four children, if they are living at my death, both personal and real estate divided equal; if not living, give share to their children. And if she is living, you must take care of your Mammy. Now this is my last will and testament. Witness my hand and seal.

James L. Chaffin
This January 16, 1919.

Although most states today require that two witnesses be present in order for a will to be considered valid, during the early part of the twentieth century North Carolina had no such criteria, and a will was considered legitimate as long as it was written in the testator's own hand, which, in James Chaffin's case, numerous witness were ready to testify that it was. Why was the Genesis 27 referenced by James Chaffin? Why had it played so prominent a role in his decision to reverse his earlier will?

That chapter of the Old Testament is the story of a wrongful inheritance and how much devastation such an act can wreak. The narrative of Jacob receiving his father Isaac's blessing instead of Esau, and the everlasting consequences of the eldest child being disinherited, apparently left a deep impression on James. Everyone surmised that he must have read that specific portion of the Bible between 1905, when he made his original will that left everything to Marshall, the third son, and 1919, when he drew up the second will, instructing that his property and assets be equally divided among them all.

While the three brothers and Mrs. Chaffin had originally reconciled themselves—with great and unusual decorum, it must be pointed out—to the stipulations of the first will, the discovery of the second will overturned their previous grace and civility. They immediately filed suit against Marshall's widow, and she promptly countersued. The local papers in North Carolina had a field day. It was one of the most fascinating and talked-about legal cases of the day. The person who had challenged the validity of the original will was the deceased man, who had written the subsequent document himself! Skeptics and supernaturalists alike, graphology experts, and ironic newspaper writers with a taste for tongue-in-cheek reporting all weighed in with their personal perspectives and varying verdicts, some of them having great fun with the legal ruckus caused by a dead man and a dream.

Chaffin v. Chaffin was finally scheduled to be heard in the Superior Court of Davie County in December 1925. The courthouse was packed with members of the press, curious busybodies, and family and friends. Three lawyers representing the brothers and ten witnesses who were prepared to swear that the handwriting on the new will was James Chaffin's assembled in the chambers. On opening day, a jury was sworn in, and then the court adjourned for lunch.

It was at this point that someone thought of showing Marshall Chaffin's widow the actual document (why no one had thought of this before remains an eternal mystery). She immediately agreed to settle out of court; although the discussion was behind closed doors, one can surmise that she conceded that the second will was clearly written in her father-in-law's unmistakable handwriting. Her lawyers withdrew the countersuit, the jury was dismissed, all the family members were called into the judge's chambers, and by late afternoon an amicable settlement was reached, one dictated by the terms of the second will.

After that, James Chaffin's sleep remained placid and undisturbed by nocturnal visits from his deceased dad (there had been a final one just a week before the trial was about to begin), and his father never appeared in his dreams again.

~ Yitta Halberstam

A FATHER'S LEGACY

*T*t's been many years since my mother, Lola, of blessed memory, told me the story of how her deceased father visited her in a dream during the Holocaust and saved her life. I wish I could recall all the details she told me, and my memory is sketchy at best, but I do remember the most important part.

I am sure that when she had her dream my mother knew her father was already dead, even though she most likely did not witness his murder. Since it was the notorious death camp Auschwitz from which she was liberated, I am guessing that this is where he was killed. As they disembarked from the train that had brought them to the concentration camp, my mother and her family were greeted by the Angel of Death, Dr. Josef Mengele, who no doubt selected her middle-aged mother and father to take "showers" in the gas chambers. They were never seen again.

My mother was a teenager at the time and was deemed capable of doing grueling, endless labor on starvation rations, and thus she was spared.

My mother told me that one day she decided that it would be advantageous if she could get a "job" in the camp kitchen. She figured that if she worked there, she could sneak out some extra food for herself and her relatives who were still alive. My mother had two sisters who came to Auschwitz with her, but eventually they succumbed to the diseases that ravaged the camps. One morning she woke up to find her sister lying cold and lifeless next to her. I don't know if one or both were alive when she resolved to find work in the kitchen, a goal she was sure could help save others.

Nor do I know how it was that she could even "apply" for that job, when she had already been assigned elsewhere. I recall that at some point during her internment, she sewed or repaired uniforms for the Germans, but we—the children of the survivors—had taken upon ourselves an eleventh commandment when it came to our parents: we didn't ever ask questions about their experiences in the Holocaust. We had to be satisfied with whatever morsels of memory they offered us. Questions they were not ready to deal with might have ripped open the extremely thin scabs that barely prevented their psychological wounds from opening and their pain gushing out. Extreme anguish and grief roiled beneath the surface of their memories. That is why my own recollection of the story is so faint.

My mother told me that the night before she planned to approach the Germans in charge of the kitchen to ask if she could work there, her father came to her in a dream as she fitfully slept on the wooden board that served as her bed. He warned her not to go.

"My child," he said in Yiddish to his baby girl, "do not go *near* the kitchen." As hungry as she may have been, she took her father's warning to heart. Either the next day, or later that week, all the Jews who worked in the kitchen were randomly rounded up by the Nazis and sent to the gas chambers. Perhaps the commander's soup had been too salty.

My mother was the only one of her immediate family to survive. Her older brother had been shot while trying to leave the ghetto. Blue-eyed and blond, he tried to pass as a gentile, but as he walked away, a former classmate, a Pole, pointed him out to a Nazi soldier. My uncle, who I guess was about twenty-one years old, was shot in the back.

My mother was the little twig that regrew her family tree out of the ashes of the Holocaust. When she died, she left three children—two named after her mother and father—thirteen grandchildren, and several great-grandchildren, whose numbers have grown since her passing.

Her father saved her life, and she in return honored her parents with the ultimate tribute. She created generations to whom she passed down her parents' legacy—both physically and spiritually. Single-handedly, she "lengthened their days" and ensured the continuation of the family line.

But if her father had not appeared to her in the dream, none of this would have happened.

~ Cheryl Kupfer

THE CROSSROADS

First Lieutenant John Carwell Anderton was in France during the spring of 1944 when he received news from his wife back home in the States that he was to become a father. The young lieutenant with General Patton's army was overjoyed at the idea of coming home after the war to his wife, Ruth, and their first child. But on February 19, 1945, near Biesdorf, Germany, the jeep in which he was riding ran over a land mine and exploded, killing everyone on board.

The twenty-one-year-old soldier—who had loved playing basketball so much that as a boy he had earned the nickname "Hotshot," or just "Hot"—would never come home. His parents, who lived in a small Tennessee town, were advised via telegram that their only son had been killed, and the news broke their heart and spirit. Of course, many friends, neighbors, and relatives in the small community had also received similar telegrams during World War II. There was enough grief to go around. No one wanted to speak of the losses of the young men of the county, or the dreadful experiences the surviving veterans had undergone. People were silent as they tried to pick up the threads that had unraveled. What words could be said to sum up the enormity of their pain, their loss? So no one spoke much about such matters, and life went on.

Ruth Anderton was now a young widow, and when her child was born in November, she named the boy after his father,

John C. Anderton Jr. She called him Johnny. The pain of the loss made it difficult for Ruth to speak to her small son about his father, and so the subject of his death, which brought only tears and sadness, was consistently avoided as the young boy grew up. His grandparents also could not bring themselves to talk about J. Carwell Sr. either, except to tell his son that his father was a soldier and had been killed in the war. Johnny eventually stopped asking the questions that seemed to cause his mother and grandparents so much pain.

After Johnny graduated from college, he began once more to look for answers, and he decided to travel to Luxembourg to visit the American veterans' cemetery where his father had been buried. He walked away, passing the neat long rows of crosses. He was still plagued by the questions that no one had wanted to answer: How did his father die, what was he like, what kind of person was his dad? These questions haunted him incessantly.

Johnny grew up, moved to the big city, started a career. Johnny and I met, got married, and had beautiful children. But despite all these blessings, my husband felt something was missing; a big void dwelled in his heart. He still had questions about his dad.

Near retirement, Johnny and I moved back to the small town where he had been raised. His mother, Ruth, and his grandparents had passed, and many of their contemporaries were gone too. It seemed as if there was no longer anyone to ask who might know anything much about John Sr. Still, Johnny didn't give up hope. He constantly prayed to God, asking that somehow his questions might be answered and that God might finally grant him peace and closure. After all these years, he still longed to know how his father had lived and how he had died, too. Who could tell him about the man he had called "Dad" but never known as a father?

Not long after we moved back to Johnny's old hometown, a Mr. Dickerson—who had grown up in Florence, Alabama, but had moved to Nashville to go into the restaurant business—also decided to return to his childhood roots. Since he too was now retired, Mr. Dickerson and his wife started taking a series of day trips in southern Tennessee and northern Alabama, revisiting the countryside of his youth. One day, with no particular destination in mind, they started down a highway until they came to a crossroads. They decided to flip a coin to determine the direction they would take. The coin was tossed, and off they went, filled with adventure and high spirits. They had absolutely no idea where the road would lead them.

Around lunchtime, they passed through a small village, Winchester, Tennessee, with which they were unfamiliar, and as they slowly traversed the main street, staring with curiosity at the vestiges of small-town America, they noticed an old sign advertising "Anderton Seed and Feed" printed on the side of a building. An uncommon name, to be sure. They stopped the car and wandered inside, asking if the owners knew if the principals of Anderton Seed and Feed were in any way related to an Anderton who had been killed in the war in 1944? The shopkeeper said that he didn't know and the Andertons who had owned the business were deceased, but there were a few families bearing that name still living in the county. Dickerson was welcome to look in the phone book, the owner offered. Mr. Dickerson scanned the directory and randomly dialed a number.

"Hello," he introduced himself. "I'm looking for some information. Are you by any chance related to a J. C. Anderton, known as 'Hot,' who served in C Company of the Fifteenth Army in France in World War II?" Mr. Dickerson asked.

"Yes, sir, that was my father. But he died in Germany in 1945. He was killed before I was born. I never knew him, though I wish I did. I've tried, but I'm afraid I haven't been able to learn anything about him. I'm sorry, but I won't be able to help you," Johnny replied.

"Well, son, that's OK, because I think that *I'll* be able to help you. You see, 'Hot' and I served together. He was my lieutenant and well loved by the whole company. I was there the day he died. He was my best friend. I'd like to tell you about him."

My husband and I met with Mr. Dickerson and had a long talk, which was deeply beneficial to both men. It seems that right after retirement, Mr. Dickerson had started thinking a lot about his war experiences, and the remembrances of his best friend "Hot" Anderton—who was killed before his eyes—had literally been haunting his dreams.

Mr. Dickerson told Johnny that "Hot" had been thrilled at the news of his wife's pregnancy and was happily looking forward to the end of the war and starting a career in the ministry when he got home. Mr. Dickerson had often wondered about the welfare of the baby with no father; he had felt compelled over the years to find out his fate, but had been unsuccessful. A crossroads and a casual toss of a coin had led to this emotional reunion, some fifty years in the making.

That day, when the two men met and exchanged their stories, there seemed to be a benevolent spirit in the room so palpable that it could only have been love itself, providing closure for two men with questions.

~ *Cheryl Anderton*

BUILDING FROM THE BROKEN PIECES

My mother-in-law, Virginia, was a beautiful woman. She exercised every day. The Bible describes Sarah at age 127 as having the beauty of a twenty-year-old. My mother-in-law's example taught me how that could be so. In her late seventies she had the gait and posture of a young woman, and she always dressed in a classic style. Her astrological sign was Leo, and she had the lion's blond "mane" and strength. Her husband, Alexander, was a serious man with a sad history, and I always felt that Virginia was the joy and sunshine that he deserved to live out his life with.

My father-in-law died first (in 2006), but we reassured ourselves that Virginia would live to a ripe old age. But five years after Alexander's death, Virginia was stricken with pancreatic cancer. My husband flew to California, where she lived, to care for her, and when school let out I joined him with our kids. Virginia's attitude was always positive, and she never complained. In private, though, she did share some of her fears with me. Virginia was a woman who had kept her house meticulously clean and who never missed a day of exercise, and she was terrified of not being able to care for herself. Of everything, the fear that loomed the largest for her was whether she would become so incapacitated that she would eventually become incontinent and lose control of her bowels. She was such a clean, elegant woman; how could she become reduced to this? When she confided her worries to her personal physician, this was his beautiful answer: "Well, when you came into this world you couldn't take care of yourself, and it was all right then."

There were so many sacred moments in her final journey. During a visit with her one day, she said to me, "I hope that wherever I'm going next, there will be work to do. I so love to work."

I tentatively asked her, "If you can . . . and if they let you . . . and if you want to . . . when you get to the Next World, would you send me a message about what it's like there?"

She smiled weakly, "You know, you're not the only one who's asked me that."

It was time for me to return home with my son, several continents away. "Well," she looked deeply into my eyes, "I guess I'll see you in the next lifetime or the Next World." The final, tearful good-bye was heart-wrenching for us both. I guess she knew then that her time was running out. Virginia's soul slipped out of her body in the quiet of night a few days later.

Afterward, I fervently waited for a dream in which she would appear, and hoped that she would at least send me a sign that she was okay—*something*. It wasn't until months later that she finally did come to me in a dream. It was vivid and bright.

We were in a workroom that was something like a very clean garage but painted all white. There was a table in the middle of the room, and on the table was a kind of boxy machine. Virginia, looking healthy and vibrant, wordlessly showed me a white box of broken shards. They were a mix of many different colors and materials. She poured the box of shards into the top of the machine, and from the bottom of the machine emerged the most magnificent mosaic vase. There are really no words to describe the otherworldly beauty of the way the pieces fit together. The shape was asymmetrical, and it did not appear to me that a vase like that could exist in this world. The pieces of the mosaic were suspended and held together by a force that was not visible to the eyes. I was in awe.

Then Virginia turned to me. "Take this with you," she said and encouraged me to pick up that mystical white box. I looked at it and answered, "It's too big!"

"No, it's not," she answered as she handed me a now-shrunk version of the box, about the size of a gift box that would contain a shirt. I reached out to receive the box, and the dream dissolved.

To me, the message of the dream was clear: the gift is that in this world of broken pieces, we can take the fragments of our lives and even the shattered lives of others and transform them into exquisite and otherworldly vessels. There is an invisible force that holds us, our dreams, our visions, our mistakes and triumphs, our very existence together. The gift of that dream visit was the knowledge that all the broken pieces of our lives are being put together on all levels, even if we can't discern that lesson on this earthly plane. But when we get to the Next World, all the shattered shards merge to create a beautiful work of art: the human beings we once were, now completely whole and no longer broken.

~ *Laya Saul*

FIXING THINGS

*M*y father was a simple man born in 1915. After serving in the US Army during World War II, he received training to become a TV technician. He was good at electronics and at fixing things in general. He was a playful and kind man who had a friendly greeting for everyone. Although he would tell his children stories—mainly about his life growing up or his army experience—in general he was like most men of his generation: more on the quiet side. The words he did share were thoughtful and deep, and I still see his influence in my life every day.

After my father's death at the glorious age of ninety-five, I hoped for a dream visit. I was pretty disappointed when month after month passed with no dream. And then it happened.

I was in the foyer of a huge office building. The entire place glistened with smooth marble. People hurriedly rushed about in the usual frenzied manner of office workers with appointments to keep and job assignments to complete. Then I saw him. In the dream, my father was young again. His hair was dark and wavy. He was tall and handsome, wearing his technician uniform and carrying his tool case.

I was so happy to see him, and I desperately wanted to hug him and talk to him, but even as I pursued him, he kept walking away from me toward the elevator. As he walked past me he said, "I have to go—I'm fixing things upstairs."

It was a short dream. I really wanted more of my father, but when I awoke the message was clear: my family has an advocate "upstairs." But that was not the only gift of that dream. My mother had been experiencing a fading memory when my father was still alive, but two years after my father's death, her dementia had become severe. During one of my visits with her she suddenly asked about my father. She said she hadn't seen him in a long time. She wondered where he was or if he had left her. It can be traumatic to tell someone with Alzheimer's about a death they don't remember; they can feel the initial grief all over again. But since that dream, I've been blessed to be able to tell my mother the complete truth.

Now, whenever she asks where her husband of sixty-eight years is, I'm able to honestly answer her, "He's out fixing things." It's an answer that satisfies us both.

~ *Laya Saul*

TEXT MESSAGES AND PHONE CALLS

FROM HEAVEN

*T*t appears that a cell phone is the tool that my deceased brother Dean finds useful for communicating with us—his loved ones whom he has left behind. During his lifetime, Dean was always into the latest gadgets. He had to have the newest smartphone as soon as the updated version hit the market. So it should have been no surprise to me that he continued using "advanced technology" as his medium of communication after he passed on.

His first message came only a few days after his funeral. Our family was at the cemetery tending to his grave. My parents and Dean's children were all there with me as we went about lighting his epitaph candle, burning incense, and saying prayers. At the gravesite, my mother's cell phone suddenly beeped, letting her know that a message had been received.

My mother was a little technologically challenged, as older people can be. She knew very little about her phone, and used it only to make and receive calls, nothing more advanced than that. The one and only time she had ever received a text message before that day had been from Dean, just prior to his death. She didn't even know how to retrieve a text, so she handed her phone to me, asking me to access the message and read it to her. I saw the message, shivered, and read it out loud: "I love you." It was unsigned and from an untraceable sender. Dean was dead. How could he be sending us a message now? We looked at each other in shock, utterly bewildered, yet undeniably sensing both Dean's presence and his love.

We are rational people, and after we recovered from the shock, it was clear to all of us that somehow someone we did not know had punched in a wrong number, and sent that message to us precisely at the moment when we sought to connect with Dean at his grave. Despite the fact that we knew it was a mistake, we still believed that the message was meant for *us*. It made us feel Dean's love and his presence. That short message gave us a great feeling of comfort that Dean was still near. It was a wrong number, but it came at the right time.

But it has not only been through text messages that Dean has used the phone to keep in touch. In 2001, just before he died, Dean gave me his old phone to use when he acquired a newer one. It had a feature that allowed you to type in a melody, note by note, for the ringtone. Among others, I entered the chorus of the old Dusty Springfield song "You Don't Have to Say You Love Me" and started to use it as my default tone. A few days before Dean died, he and I were sitting around our campsite, and Dean was going through my phone, listening to the various songs I had chosen. He seemed to be listening most intently to the Dusty Springfield song. But for some reason, right after that night I changed the default ringtone to an entirely different tune from my library.

After Dean died, I was grieving very hard, looking for ways to understand his death, wishing I had told him more often how much he meant to me. One day, when I was particularly consumed by my raw grief and guilt that I hadn't expressed my love for him as frequently as I should have, my phone rang, but it *did not* play the ringtone I had set. It played the Dusty Springfield song instead. How had this happened? Until that moment, it had consistently rung with the new tone I had chosen. Why had it suddenly reverted to the Dusty Springfield melody when I was especially immersed in my ruminations about Dean? It had never malfunctioned before. I could not see this as anything other than an intervention by Dean himself to pass on a message to me.

The Dusty Springfield song—which beseeches a loved one who has left to stay close—was one that I would end up singing repeatedly to help me come to terms with what had happened.

This phone originally belonged to Dean. He had listened to that tune with rapt attention. It seemed clear that he was looking to tell me that the message I had gleaned from the song was the message he wanted me to hear from him—that he was close.

Here in Australia, most of us are used to getting alerts from our cell phones to call our MessageBank® (a service in which voice mails are converted to text messages) when it contains a new, unread message. Exactly on the eighth anniversary of Dean's death, I received one of these messages. What unsettled me, however, was the strange fact that while I definitely heard an alert that a text message had appeared, my phone did not show any missed calls. Neither had I heard the phone ring. Still, according to my phone, I *did* have a new, unread message. I called the MessageBank service to retrieve the message I had received, only to discover there was nothing there! But while there may have been no message on the phone, I felt I had received one, nonetheless. It was clear to me that it was my brother who had left the message, letting me know he was there as best he could. People might chalk it up to a malfunction, but to me it is difficult to explain how such an inexplicable error could have occurred precisely on the anniversary of Dean's death. The MessageBank had never malfunctioned before, nor did it after.

I don't know when I will receive another message, but I do know with certainty that if Dean wants to contact me again, the phone is definitely one of the mediums through which he will get in touch!

~ *Anna Rawlings*

THE NUMBER 38

My brother Dean's favorite number was 38. It appeared in his life a lot. Coincidentally, when he died, he was exactly 38 years old. After his death, I also started seeing this number *everywhere*.

For example, whenever I looked at my watch or the clock on the wall, inevitably the time would be 38 minutes past the hour. The number 38 would be displayed as part of a car registration, be the designated table where I was placed in restaurants, appear on ticket numbers, and so on. It seemed to continuously pop up in my life, and it would constantly remind me of my brother, keeping the connection between us alive.

When I felt that my son was old enough to spend time in day care, I decided that it was time to do something for myself. I chose to build on my interest in art and signed up for a course in visual arts. As I progressed through the course, I felt the need to exhibit my work. One of the other students brought in leaflets about an exhibition called *Nowa Nowa Nudes*, a well-established art competition.

I struggled for ideas about what to paint for the exhibition. My husband and I wanted to have a second baby, and one afternoon when we were lying in bed, inspiration struck. I quickly drew some outlines of my idea, which then developed into the final artwork. My work was entitled *Trying to Conceive*—as that was the basis for my inspiration—and it got into the show, along with several hundred works by other artists. Since this was the first time my artwork was being publically exhibited, my husband and I decided to travel the two-hour distance to the event to view the works on display, mine among them. As we entered the exhibition hall and were given a catalog, my eyes scanned the titles, looking for my entry. To my amazement and thrill I had been allocated number 38! We wandered around the various rooms searching for my piece, until finally we found it. There it was . . . sitting proudly on the wall, bearing a sticker with the number 38.

Of course, I saw this as very auspicious, and it crossed my mind that perhaps Dean's signature imprint might mean that I was to win the competition, or that something else of import would occur related to the event. But that was not to be. However, I still felt a deep connection to my brother and believed he was showing support for what I was doing; he was letting me know he was here again.

My husband and I had been trying to conceive a baby for some time, and each month I had to deal with the disappointment when I didn't become pregnant. Shortly after the art exhibit, I was showering one night when a thought crossed my mind: "Wouldn't it be a beautiful thing if I were pregnant this month, the month I saw the number 38." Once again I would feel that Dean was around and happy for me. However, I didn't want to get my hopes up.

For that cycle my menstrual period was due to start on November 11, which is commemorated as Remembrance Day in Australia. So on Remembrance Day, a day when we remember all those who lost their lives in wars, I took a pregnancy test and found out that yes, indeed, I was pregnant.

I felt then that both the inspiration for my artwork and the title were Dean's way of telling me that the pregnancy was going to happen. The number 38 randomly being chosen as the number for my exhibit clearly told me that Dean was giving me a message. It was not Dean making my art win. It was Dean sharing in the joy of our special news that our baby was on its way.

The coincidence of my artwork creation, the entry number, and my pregnancy seemed to lead to only one conclusion: my brother knew I was pregnant before I did. And he just couldn't wait to share the news.

~ *Anna Rawlings*

HELLO, LYNN

When my mother was dying, I asked her to let me know when she got to the other side. She nodded and rolled her eyes with motherly indulgence. She feared she was going to an empty, black void.

Less than two months after she passed, I attended a computer workshop with thirty other members of the library staff. It was held on October 3, which would have been her eighty-seventh birthday.

I arrived early and sat at a computer in the back of the room. When I moved the mouse, a slate green screen came up. "Hello, Lynn" was written in pale, swooping script.

I wondered how the technical staff had programmed the computer to do this and how they knew which seat I would choose.

I looked around. The people on my left were casually chatting. The seats to my right were empty. I didn't overhear anyone asking, "Is there a personal greeting on your computer?"

I looked back. The message was still there. I smiled and whispered, "Hello." I was willing to play along, even though I didn't recognize the game or know the rules. During the workshop I would hear that arguing with the computer or even talking to it is called "having an emotional relationship with a machine."

As I listened to the instructor's opening remarks, the waving parabolas on my screen saver returned. When we were asked to begin working, the standard library home page came up. The "Hello, Lynn" screen was gone. I tried to get it back, but I never found it again. Later I would realize that no slate green screen existed anywhere on the library computers, and the screen I saw looked an awful lot like the blackboards my mother had once written on during her years as a teacher.

For months, I was afraid to tell anyone. Would people think I was nuts? I stewed about it until Karin, one of my colleagues at Project Second Chance (a literacy program), told me about the spirit of her grandfather. Karin was a pragmatic woman, and I was surprised to hear her describe a long-dead grandfather who played with the volume on the radio and dropped spoons in the kitchen. Her story gave me chills. It also gave me courage.

In a trembling voice, I told her about the screen with "Hello, Lynn" that appeared on my mother's birthday.

"Nice of her to drop by," Karin said.

Even so, it took me several years to realize this was my mother's way of telling me that she was on the other side and everything was all right.

~ *B. Lynn Goodwin*

ༀ ཙ

DRIVING THROUGH THE STORM

*T*he sense of "mystery" that permeates so many people's lives never ever touched mine. I experienced mystery only vicariously through my teenage Nancy Drew books, and "magical" was the way I felt, when, as a small child, I held a sparkle-tipped wand bought at the annual performance of the touring circus. In other words, unearthly or mystical occurrences were unknown quantities in my personal world. Sure, some schoolmates carried four-leaf clovers pressed into small glass key-ring circles and fingered them during tests, and a few had silky rabbit's-foot chains dangling from the shoulder strap of their purses. I often listened to the LP of the Broadway show *Guys and Dolls*, which featured a song with lyrics that pleaded for luck to be a lady, but it was the music I liked, not its message. Fate, chance, or something else from beyond this world—none of these things held any import for me or figured in my life. The early 1950s filled me with education and a special sense of self, and childhood dreams became tiny teenage realities, but not because of anything so ethereal as "luck." My parents made me feel secure and important through their unconditional caring; no matter how hard I leaned on them, they didn't even tilt.

Mystery took on its real meaning of something impossible to explain when, one month after my springtime twentieth birthday, my forty-five-year-old father died of a heart attack. How could his body, clothed by a shroud, not move? How could a pine box so narrow contain a man who filled the air with kindness and sensitivity and smiles, no matter what was going on inside him? Where was "he"? How could I need to use the bathroom when time should just stop as his heart had! I screamed aloud, "Don't hurt him!" as ropes lowered that box into Long Island's reddish soil.

The train took me back to college in Connecticut, and I completed my junior year. During the winter of my senior year, I was with a date; we'd gone to see a live performance in a theater in Hartford, about forty-five minutes from campus via a country road. A sudden storm created driving conditions that frightened my date as he struggled to keep the auto from sliding off the slick road while trying to focus on the windshield, which snow covered as quickly as the rubber wipers cleared the glass. He was a nervous wreck, but I was preternaturally calm. I was so quiet, in fact, that my date thought I'd blacked out. "Anyone else would be screaming!" he almost yelled as his fingers continued to grip the steering wheel. His voice was shrill with the high pitch of doom. In contrast, I was not gripped with fear of the car sliding into one of New England's massive old trees, or of a car behind us not seeing pale taillights, or even the threat of a rollover. I felt absolutely no concern for our safety and was serene.

Was my date sure we were headed for disaster as we veered across the road? Was he muttering a prayer because he thought we were going to die? Even as he finally gained control of the car and got us safely back to campus, he still remained severely shaken, and his feeling of the near disaster we had averted impacted him hard. This close brush with mortality made him shudder.

I gently touched his arm. He looked at me strangely as he thanked me for not upsetting him more by screaming at him or clutching him while we were on the road. "You were . . . ," he hesitated and then finished his sentence, "great," but he also seemed utterly bewildered by my mysterious composure. "Any other girl would have been in tears by now—either from the fright of it all or from the sheer relief. How can you be so calm?" he finally demanded.

"I just knew that my father was with me," I said. "It was the strongest sense. And I knew he wouldn't let anything happen to us, just as he wouldn't allow my mother to suffer by burying another loved one."

"How could you be so sure your father was with you?" my date asked. "Are you sure it wasn't your imagination?"

I was not dreaming. My dad was there. The distinct scent of his signature aftershave lotion (which my date did not use) had inexplicably filled the car even as it swerved across the road. Prior to the storm and the car veering almost out of control, the car had been odor-free.

My dad had always protected me, and he was protecting me now. I truly knew that his soul was there in the car with me that night and that it was not just my imagination. An extremely devoted father and husband, he made sure to keep his twenty-year-old daughter safe. By so doing, he also shielded his cherished wife from the horrific suffering that a phone call about a car crash involving her daughter would clearly have engendered.

All these decades later, I've never had that profound experience again. Sometimes I vaguely sense my father's presence and smile, thinking he's still protecting me after so many years, but I've never felt it as powerfully and with such certainty as I did that night. It was the only time I ever felt engulfed by his smell. It could not have been a dream, or even a "vision," and I know my memory has not embellished the story with the passage of time, because that very night, back in my dorm, I wrote down everything that had just occurred. I penned a letter of thanks to my father, just "in case" he could read it. I wanted him to know that *I* knew it was because of him that I was safe. I have that letter still.

It might be argued that I probably imagined the scent of my father's aftershave, but in the midst of such high drama and near catastrophe, I can't believe I would suddenly become so fanciful. For me, it was clearly a "small miracle," definitely divine, and to this day it fills me with the great sense of mystery that had eluded me before that incident.

~ *Lois Greene Stone*

A HURRICANE SANDY MIRACLE

It was October 29, 2012, two hours before high tide, when Hurricane Sandy was predicted to hit the northeast Atlantic coast. A quick look out the back door of our house revealed a four-and-a-half-foot sheet of water extending to a smaller canal about two hundred yards to the west.

As the flood surged to mid-calf level, my boyfriend and I began moving emergency supplies into the attic, along with Bogart the cat. We lifted cat food, litter, water, blankets, a first-aid kit, power bars, laptops, a TV screen, and a backup drive to safety, along with candles, lanterns, matches, and an emergency radio/lantern that operated on electricity, batteries, solar power, and a crank. My boyfriend had laughed at me when I had proudly unpacked this last item, after buying it from Macy's the previous May as a birthday present to myself. He was not laughing now.

Nor was he laughing at the gallons of water I had stockpiled. Five months earlier, in May 2012, my father had appeared to me in a dream. "Buy water," he said. "You are going to need it." My dad died in 1989, but I figured if he had gone to the trouble of showing up in a dream, I needed to pay attention. Each time I went to the supermarket, I would grab a gallon of water to take home. After I had stockpiled half a dozen gallons, I was forced to admit that I had, in fact, become something of a closet prepper.

But not enough of a prepper. At least not according to my Uncle Nick, who had died in 1991. Six weeks after my father's spirit appeared in my dream, Uncle Nick showed up, sitting in a wing chair and smoking his signature cherry tobacco in his favorite pipe. "Laur, you are not taking this seriously. You really need to buy more water."

"Okay, Uncle Nick," I said in my dream. Waking up with firm resolve, I made it back from the store with another three gallons. Surely, nine gallons was enough!

But my father was not pleased. He returned that Labor Day, standing tall in my dream and giving me his "Young lady, I am not pleased!" expression. He said, "Laurie, you need to pay attention. You do not have enough water, and you are going to need it." I still had no idea what he was talking about, but I dutifully lugged in another four gallons, bringing the grand total to thirteen gallons of water.

All thirteen gallons were now lined up on the kitchen counter, along with three cartons of one-liter bottles. I still couldn't understand why my dad's and uncle's spirits had come back to tell me to get water. We had more than enough! As the floodwaters reached three and a half feet, they lifted the refrigerator off the ground. Carried by the swell, it crashed into the washing machine, which was also afloat. A six-foot leather coach was pushed into the doorway of the living room.

When the flood was chest high, we climbed the stairs into the attic, where we peered down to watch the water make its way up the stairs. We managed to fall asleep for a couple of hours, waking up when we heard voices outside. The tide had receded, leaving an oily film on the tile floor. A few hours later, we realized that everything in the house was smeared with raw sewage. During the surge, the town's sewer pump had broken. Our water supply was contaminated.

Now I understood why my father and my uncle had journeyed from the spirit world to make sure I had plenty of water!

Even though everything I had built over the previous twenty years had been wiped out in less than an hour, I smiled and thanked them for taking care of me.

~ *Laurie Nadel*

LILA AND LOLO

*T*hey were as close as twins, two siblings born less than a
year apart in Cienfuegos, a city in Cuba.

She, Maria Amelia, was born in 1921, and he, Eduardo, in
1922. As children, she was called Lila and he was called Lolo,
so Lila and Lolo they remained all their lives. They even looked
alike, except that in old age he had no hair, while she, until
her final breath, had thick, rich tresses. One time Lolo popped
on a wig, and he looked exactly like his sister (but without the
makeup).

My wife was Lila's daughter and Lolo's niece. She loved her
uncle dearly, and he, childless during fifty-seven years of marriage, adored her. When Liliana, my wife, was just eleven, in
1960, her parents took her and her sister out of Cuba because of
the revolution. Sadly, Lolo's allegiance to the revolution divided
the family, and he and his wife remained in Cuba.

By the 1990s, relations between the United States and Cuba
had eased, and as retirees Lolo and his wife were able to visit us
in Florida a couple of times. We, in turn, took our two daughters and spent two weeks in Cuba with them in 1997, including
celebrating their fiftieth wedding anniversary.

By 2004, Lila had severe Alzheimer's and was hanging on
to life even though she really had no remaining quality of life;
every day we were amazed that she still survived. Her tormented
daughters could not understand how she continued to live with

almost no ability to communicate or, often, even to recognize them. It was a sad time for the family.

Lolo knew about his sister's condition, but unbeknownst to my wife, he himself (who had always been robust) had developed a heart condition that had weakened him terribly. One morning in October, when he awoke, he told his wife that it was time for him to rest, and he breathed his last.

When the phone call came from Cuba a few minutes later with the news of his death, my wife was distraught. She was plunged into a deep sadness at losing her beloved uncle (to her, his death was very unexpected), and she felt terribly guilty that she had not made more of an effort to visit him again in Cuba. I have never seen her so sad. I asked her if she wanted me to stay home with her, but she urged me to go to work; she said she would drive to the home of some dear Cuban friends and spend time with them. I wasn't sure that was the best idea, but she seemed determined.

So it happened that still weeping on the morning of her uncle's death, Liliana ended up driving on the interstate in a deluge of tropical rain—tears inside and outside the car, as it were. Suddenly, in a corner of the windshield, like a small reflection, the image of her uncle appeared, and he began to talk with her. And, unbelievably, somehow—while driving through rain and speeding semis—she found paper and a pencil and kept notes on the conversation.

It was a long and detailed conversation, but the principal topics were these: Lolo told her how sad he was to cause her this heartbreak, but that he was exhausted and that it was his time. He told her not to feel guilty about the fact that she had not recently visited Cuba because she had so many worries and concerns about her own mother's final days. He said, "My sister is afraid to die. You and Diana (my wife's sister) have been tormented about her, but now try to let that anguish go. Now I will be able to help her."

When the conversation ended, my wife pulled off the interstate into a gas station and called me and read me what they had talked about. The conversation had seemed totally natural and very specific, and it contained information from him about the family that she had not known before. More than that, all her sadness was gone; it was replaced by a sense of peace and calm.

True to his word, Lila, Lolo's sister, finally died from her Alzheimer's, just one month, one day, and one hour after her brother Lolo's death.

~ Bill Cunningham

THE PERFECT GIFT

Sarah grew up as part of a large and loving family in England. Although her parents didn't have much money, Sarah did not feel deprived. Her hardworking and devoted parents mastered the art of parenting; they had many ways of showing their eleven children that each and every one of them was cherished and beloved.

Sarah's father was a well-respected scholar and community leader with many different obligations that often called him away from home. Nevertheless, his children always knew that they were important to him. Before retiring late every evening, he went from room to room to make sure that all his children were well covered and warm. During the summer holidays he would join in the children's games with great enthusiasm and playfulness. Once he even helped them build a stone dam over a creek in the countryside. No matter how busy he was, Sarah knew just how precious she was to her father.

Sarah's mother was a very dignified woman who had grown up in a wealthy home. She was intelligent and talented and at one time had even held down a high-profile job. But as her family grew, she relinquished her career for the sake of her family. She had a knack for creating beautiful clothing out of affordable fabrics, and she saw to it that she and her children were well dressed and put together. Not only did she provide for her children's physical needs, Sarah's mother also made sure to provide for their emotional needs as well. In order to give her children individual attention, she would take them one at a time on monthly outings. The children always knew that she was available to them should they want to talk to her about anything.

Sarah married, and she and her husband had several children. After ten years of marriage, they moved abroad, where they built their own home. Even though thousands of miles now separated Sarah and her parents, they were still very much an integral part of her life. She called them regularly, and her mother's love and wisdom accompanied her throughout her childbearing years. Despite her physical absence, her mother remained an important presence in Sarah's life, and she continued to take as much care of Sarah as was possible from overseas.

A decade later, Sarah's mother passed away suddenly. Three days after her mother's death, Sarah gave birth to a little girl. She was deeply pained at the thought of being so far away from her family—her father and her siblings—at this crucial time. She wanted to be with them and mourn together, but both her circumstances (having just given birth) as well as the considerable geographical distance that separated them made it impossible for her to join them.

Six years after her mother's death, Sarah was blessed with another baby girl. As every woman who has given birth knows, the postpartum period is often a time of great emotional vulnerability. Every feeling, no matter how fleeting, is magnified to great proportions. In Sarah's case, the scab that had covered the loss of her mother six years earlier opened up and became a raw wound once again. It was precisely when Sarah became a mother yet again that she ached for her own mother's love more than ever before. Now that she had given birth, she yearned for her mother incessantly, desperately needing her tenderness and counsel, her nurturing and wisdom.

And then—just a few days later—she received the shock of her life when a parcel arrived in the mail addressed to her in the familiar handwriting of her mother! How could this be? Stunned and overcome with emotion, Sarah undid the parcel, which astoundingly contained clothing for a baby girl!

Sarah was so taken aback that she burst out laughing, though she was also crying at the same time. It just didn't make sense. How could Sarah's mother send her a baby gift *six years* after she had died?

After doing some detective work, this is what she turned up: Upon the birth of Sarah's eldest daughter some twenty years earlier, her mother had apparently prepared a package of baby clothing that she entrusted to a woman who was visiting the UK. The package was addressed to Sarah in her mother's handwriting, ready for the woman to mail as soon as she arrived overseas, where Sarah lived. But then, inexplicably, the "courier" placed the package on a shelf in her home and completely forgot about it for the next twenty years! Now the woman was in the process of moving from her home and had stumbled across the mislaid package as she emptied her shelves. An ethical woman, she felt remorse that she had forgotten her original assignment, and she decided that there was nothing for her to do other than finally follow through on her commitment to mail the package.

And that's how Sarah came to receive the perfect gift from her departed mother precisely when she needed it the most.

~ Penina Neiman

ANGELS IN GO-GO BOOTS

When I was eight years old, my mother and I were in a terrible car accident on I-95 in Greenwich, Connecticut. It happened in the late afternoon on a beautiful summer day in August 1962. I had spent the day playing in our backyard with my friends, doing somersaults and cartwheels on the grass and relaxing on the swing my father had built for his children in a big maple tree.

Later that day, my mother and I left the house to pick up my older brother from the beach so we could drop him off for his paper route. From there, we planned to drive to a store in Greenwich to buy an iron. This was in the days when mothers still ironed, and the kids in the neighborhood roamed freely from one yard to another, without much adult supervision. My dad was in the Navy Reserve, training somewhere in the Midwest, and when he was away my mother liked to say, "When the cat's away, the mice will play!" (meaning the ability to shop freely).

But my mother wasn't her usual merry self that hot August afternoon despite the pleasures of being on her own. My brother wasn't waiting for her at the beach as they had originally arranged, and she was worried.

Well . . . maybe he got impatient waiting for us and hitched a ride home with someone else, or maybe he took the bus, she thought as she tried to reassure herself. We were late, after all, so she couldn't fault him for not hanging around.

My mother swung the car into reverse and headed toward the Connecticut turnpike en route to Greenwich.

It was sweltering hot, and we lowered the windows and let the breeze in. Our hair was wild from the wind and the heat, and my mom decided that this was a good time to teach me her favorite song, "My Baby Just Cares for Me."

We started off fairly well, but then I would always end up going off-key, and my mother would tell me to stop and start again, trying to get me to sing it right. We were both getting frustrated when suddenly she tensed and screamed at me to "shut up!" A big truck was passing. It was making a lot of noise, and I'm not really sure what happened next, but we ended up crashing into a pole. Everything seemed to go in slow motion as we crashed. I flew through the windshield as glass shattered all around me, while my mother remained trapped in the car.

The next thing I remember was lying on the grass on the side of the highway. The usual noise of traffic from the road seemed to recede, and all was quiet, but through the silence I could hear the birds chirping and feel the bright white light of the sun on my face. I looked around, and that was when I noticed that there was a fence nearby, in what seemed to be a residential area, and that just behind that fence there were two girls, a little older than me. They were just standing there, staring at me. Although they didn't speak, I could see that they were smiling at me in encouragement, and they seemed to be telling me that everything would be all right.

And then I noticed they were wearing go-go boots! Yes, go-go boots, just like the girls on *Hullabaloo*, my favorite TV show. My mind was a bit hazy and jumbled, and all I could think was, I want to wear go-go boots too! I want to live, so I can grow up and become a teenager and wear go-go boots!

And that's exactly what I did. Both my mom and I were hospitalized, and we each underwent a long recovery, but thankfully the girls were right: everything did turn out all right, after all.

But here's the miracle—I have driven along this part of I-95 for many years, and there is *no fence* there. There are no houses in the area. There is no place where these two teenage girls dressed in white could have come from!

And so I am left with the only conclusion—they were angels. And stylish angels, at that!

~ *Jamie Cat Callan*

THE SHOFAR

*R*abbi Yitzhak Finkler, the renowned Grand Rebbe of Radoszyce, was one of the great spiritual heroes of the twentieth century. In the Polish town of Pietrokov (Piotrków) where his chassidic court reigned, Rabbi Finkler had acquired a reputation as a holy man whose prayer services were unparalleled for their warmth, depth, and beauty. Multitudes traveled to his shul (synagogue), drawn by his melodious voice, spirited singing, charisma, and, above all, saintly character.

One of his most avid followers was a little boy named Moshe Waintreter; the Rebbe became the centerpiece of the boy's life. The Rebbe conferred dignity on everyone he met and always paused to give Moshe a kiss and a blessing when their paths converged. That they would intersect even more meaningfully, much later on in a labor camp, neither of them could have known in advance.

In 1943, when Moshe was twenty-nine and his parents were long dead, he was deported—without any family or friends alongside to buttress him—to the Skarzysko-Kamienna labor camp in southeastern Poland. Although labor camps were not officially classified by the Nazis as extermination camps like Treblinka or Sobibór, they were in effect run under the principle of "extermination through labor." Skarzysko-Kamienna was infamous for being a slow and certain path to death, a place where inmates were subjected to particularly brutal conditions and frequent "selections." (Perhaps one of the reasons Skar-zysko-Kamienna is little known is that so few survived it.)

This was the heinous hellhole into which Moshe Waintreter was hurled, two years before the end of the war. But incongruously, almost as soon as he entered the barracks to which he was directed—Barracks 14—something captured his eye that gave him cause for unbridled joy. It was the visage of no less than his beloved Rebbe—Rabbi Yitzhak Finkler, the Grand Rebbe of Radoszyce—who miraculously was assigned to the exact same quarters as he! Moshe was flooded with enormous relief, comforted by the Rebbe's sheer presence. But he could not help but wonder anxiously: What had these horrible years wrought? What battle scars did the Rebbe himself carry? Was he worn and tired? Was his soul battered to a pulp? Moshe exchanged a few trembling words with the Rebbe and was instantly reassured that his faith was still intact, his wings still spread out like a sheltering tent for all those who sought its refuge. And not only did the Rebbe continue to minister unstintingly to his flock, offering endless words of comfort and encouragement to the dispirited, he had also managed to turn the gray and grimy quarters of Barracks 14 into a makeshift *beit midrash* (synagogue and yeshiva), from which—as much as it was possible—the commandments were secretly practiced and holiness emanated.

Every morning, under the cover of darkness, a pair of phylacteries (*tefillin*) that had been smuggled into the camp was passed around the barracks, so that each man had the opportunity to fulfill the mitzvah (commandment). The Rebbe conducted regular Sabbath prayer services and, whenever it was possible, taught the Torah. That his teacher could continue to observe the religious precepts under the most challenging conditions was a beacon of light for Moshe, a constant source of inspiration. Everyone was continually amazed by the Rebbe's inner fortitude, by his enormous wellsprings of love, which flowed over and enveloped each man in the barracks. If they hadn't been his ardent followers before the war, they were now.

As the advent of Pesach (Passover) 1943 drew near, the Rebbe decided it was imperative that the seder be observed in some concrete, tangible way. He approached Shloma, one of his loyal congregants in Barracks 14, and asked him to undertake an important commission. He asked Shloma, who worked in the camp's kitchen, to acquire and hide enough beets so that they could make a juice substitute from them to use for the *arba kosos* (four cups of wine) during the seder.

Shloma was petrified, but the Rebbe assured him that in the merit of performing this great mitzvah, he would give Shloma his personal blessing and promised him that he would survive and live to see many better years. Like all the other religious Jews in the labor camp, Shloma revered the Rebbe. Whether he believed that the Rebbe's blessing would truly protect him was another question, but he simply could not say no to him. On a daily basis the Rebbe put his life on the line for his fellow Jews, and now it was time for Shloma to put his life on the line for the Rebbe. He performed the Rebbe's bidding, his clandestine activities mercifully undetected by the prison guards, and that Pesach, the Jews in the camp fulfilled the commandment of drinking the four cups—with Shloma's beet juice.

Despite the physical blows that Rabbi Finkler endured and the monstrous scenes of evil he was forced to watch (in one horrific episode, the Jews were ordered to grab the dead bodies of their fellows and dance with the corpses while singing in Yiddish), the Rebbe's spiritual resistance never wavered. When Rosh Hashanah loomed, he determined that a shofar (ram's horn) must be acquired to confer the High Holy Days with spiritual meaning and authenticity, to give the inmates a remembrance of those bygone times when their spirits soared heavenward. The Rebbe took a diamond he had hidden—one that could have easily bought him more food and less privation—and gave it to a local Pole who worked in the camp. "I give you this diamond in exchange for a ram's horn," he bribed the peasant. The man's eyes glinted greedily, and he grabbed the gem. A few days later, he brought the Rebbe a horn—one belonging to an ox.

"No, no!" the Rebbe expostulated. "This is not the right horn. A ram's horn is what I asked for."

"But I can't find a ram's horn around here," the peasant whined.

"Listen," the Rebbe said sternly, "if you want me to give you more diamonds in the future, you will have to find me a ram's horn. Otherwise, I will approach someone else." Several days later, the peasant returned, this time bearing a ram's horn in his pocket.

Shloma had successfully dispatched the Rebbe's assignment for Pesach, and as the Rebbe had promised, he had eluded both suspicion and punishment. But Shloma worked in the kitchen, and there were no implements in that workplace that could aid him in the fashioning of a shofar. Moshe, however, labored in a metal factory, where he could gain access to the exact tools needed.

"Moshe," the Rebbe tenderly intercepted him one morning, "I have known you since were a little boy, and I knew your father very well, too. I want to entrust you with the holy task of making a shofar from this ram's horn that was smuggled into the camp, so we can all fulfill the mitzvah of *tekias shofar* (listening to the shofar) on Rosh Hashanah. I know that you work as a craftsman, and I am sure you will have the wherewithal to make the shofar in the factory where you work."

Anguish and fear flickered in Moshe's eyes as he turned to appeal to his beloved master. "Rebbe," he said faintly, "I would love to do it, you know I would do anything for you, but just yesterday a Jew from my workplace smuggled in a tiny piece of leather that he hid in his belt. A guard inspected his clothing and, when he found the leather, shot him dead. We are checked every day as we go in and out of the factory, Rebbe. If a man was killed for a scrap of leather, surely I will be killed, too."

"Moshe," the Rebbe replied gently, using the exact same words with which he had countered Shloma's fears just six months before, when he had asked him to make the beet juice. "I understand your fear. But in the merit of this great mitzvah, I will give you my blessing and promise that you will survive and live to see many better years."

"But, Rebbe," Moshe protested weakly, "I have absolutely no idea how to fashion a shofar."

"I am sure that you will find a way," the Rebbe answered.

Unable to refuse the Rebbe's request, Moshe reluctantly set out to fulfill it. After successfully smuggling the ram's horn into the metal factory, he furtively approached several fellow Jews, asking if any of them knew how to make a shofar.

"You boil it in hot milk," one man said authoritatively.

"You dip it into cold water," another said.

There was no consensus.

Frustrated by his inability to acquire clear direction, Moshe followed his own instincts. He picked up a tool and began drilling. Within a few minutes, the factory foreman was at his side, alerted to Moshe's "subversive" activity by the very public buzzing sound of the drill.

"*What* are you doing?" the foreman demanded.

Moshe's father had once told him that the best way to disarm an interrogator was to surprise him with the truth.

"I'm making a shofar, so that we can blow it on the High Holy Days, Rosh Hashanah and Yom Kippur," he said.

"Are you crazy?" the foreman shouted, pushing Moshe into a storage room nearby.

It's over. I'm dead now. The Rebbe's blessing didn't protect me after all, Moshe thought, bracing himself for the gunshot.

But none came.

In the privacy of the empty storage room, the foreman addressed him in an entirely different voice, his demeanor suddenly gentle, in contrast to the harsh bark Moshe had heard only seconds before.

"Listen," he told Moshe, "I am a religious Catholic, and I believe in the Bible. I respect your religion, and I respect the sacrifices you religious Jews make to follow your faith. I will allow you to make your shofar. I'll lock you in here with the tools you need, so no one else will see what you're doing and you'll be safe." A few days later, Moshe slipped the crude but completely kosher shofar into the Rebbe's outstretched hands.

On Rosh Hashanah morning, before they were dispatched to work, the fervently religious congregants of Barracks 14—whose bodies had long ago been broken but whose souls remained miraculously intact—rose early to hear the last *tekias shofar* of the Grand Rebbe of Radoszyce. And although the shofar was makeshift and crude, its notes were pure and true, piercing the prisoners' hearts, penetrating Heaven, and breaking down its inner gates.

In late May 1944, as the Soviets moved west, the Nazis started to liquidate Skarzysko-Kamienna in mass killings. The few survivors who remained were deported to Czestochowa (a smaller forced labor camp nearby) or Buchenwald, Moshe Waintreter among them. Sadly, the Rebbe of Radoszyce was not. Of the 25,000 to 30,000 Jews brought to Skarzysko-Kamienna, 18,000 to 23,000 perished, among them most of the Jews from Radoszyce.

Having gotten wind of his impending deportation in advance, Moshe had enough time to return to his old barracks and ferret out the shofar from its hiding place. He managed to successfully smuggle it into Czestochowa, where he clung to the shofar as tenaciously as he clung to life itself. Even though theft among the prisoners was a sad but ongoing reality of camp life, Moshe was able, with a lot of ingenuity, to hide the shofar from both the prying eyes of his fellow inmates and the punctilious inspections of the prison guards. Each evening, Moshe would return from his labors and frantically search his secret hiding place to make sure the shofar was still there. And, miraculously, it was. Perhaps it merited special divine protection because it had belonged to the saintly Rebbe of Radoszyce, Moshe often mused, vividly remembering the exquisite, searing notes of the last blowing of this shofar, which floated heavenward from a boiling cauldron of hell. Other men in his barracks secreted their small possessions, too, Moshe knew, but none, he was sure, was as precious as the shofar, the only legacy of Rabbi Yitzhak Finkler, a legacy Moshe was determined to guard, at any cost.

One day, while he was at work, Moshe was suddenly pulled out of his spot and summarily thrown onto a train bound for Buchenwald. His heart splintered into a thousand shards. He did not wonder about the fate that awaited him in his new camp, but rather he worried about the fate of the shofar he left behind. He could not stop lamenting its loss.

When Moshe was liberated from Buchenwald in April 1945 and people began to marvel at his remarkable tale of survival, he attributed everything to the *bracha* (blessing) that he had been given by the Rebbe of Radoszyce. "I know it was the saintly Rebbe's blessing that kept me alive," he told everyone. "Only that and nothing else."

Moshe yearned to find the shofar, if it had not yet been reduced to rubble and ash, but immediately after the war humanitarian concerns took precedence. He traveled to Italy, where he participated in organizing the illegal immigration of

Jews by ship to the shores of Israel. There he met and married Ida, also a survivor. When his work in Italy was finished, the couple moved to Israel, where Moshe continued to live as a religious Jew, his faith unshaken.

Moshe settled into his new life with Ida, who gave birth to a son, and he integrated quickly and successfully into his new surroundings. Of course, all survivors bore their scars—some quietly, others more vocally—and the recent past intruded upon all of their lives, no matter how much they tried to forget. But in addition to the horrific experiences he had endured, Moshe was also haunted by the irrevocable loss of the Radoszyce shofar. The Radoszyce dynasty had been wiped out. The shofar was all that remained, the only artifact that testified to the Rebbe's valor and greatness, the one concrete symbol that bore witness to his extraordinary spiritual resistance during the Holocaust. The shofar was Moshe's sole physical link to the Rebbe, and finding it—and bringing it to Israel—was the only tangible way he could honor the Rebbe's memory and inspire people with his story. So Moshe set out to find the shofar, combing five continents—Australia, South America, North America, Europe, and the Middle East—for survivors of Czestochowa, anyone who might possibly know the fate of the shofar he had involuntarily left behind. But though he successfully tracked down several former inmates of the camp, no one knew where the shofar was.

Moshe persevered. He placed ads in Yiddish newspapers, wrote to Holocaust-survivor organizations, contacted friends of friends of friends. One of these was Vladka Meed, a former Warsaw Ghetto fighter and wife of Benjamin Meed, renowned founder and chairman of the American Gathering of Jewish Holocaust Survivors and Their Descendants. As mainstays of a nucleus to which Holocaust narratives flowed, the Meeds were often privy to obscure pieces of information no one else knew, repositories of other people's stories that weren't publicized anywhere else. One fateful day in the mid-1970s, someone casually told Vladka about a crudely made shofar that had been presented to a prominent Yiddish author when he visited the local Jewish community of Czestochowa in 1945. The newly repatriated residents of Czestochowa—those who had chosen to return to their hometown instead of emigrating somewhere else—had found the shofar in the abandoned camp and didn't know what to do with it. So they presented it to the author as a gift.

Vladka tracked down the author's widow, who still had the shofar in her possession and convinced her to part with it. Then she called Moshe and jubilantly told him that his thirty-year-long search was finally over. Since she and Benjamin had already booked tickets for an upcoming trip to Israel, they promised Moshe that they would personally deliver it to him at his home in Bnei Brak. They carefully placed the shofar in their luggage, which they checked at their airline's counter at the airport in New York.

But while the attendant was writing out the luggage tags (this was before everything was computerized), Vladka had a sudden queasy feeling. "You know," she told Benjamin, "I don't feel right about this. We shouldn't just put something as precious and holy as this shofar into our suitcase. I want to take it with me." Vladka asked the attendant to allow her to extract the shofar from the suitcase, and she placed it in her voluminous handbag instead. When the Meeds arrived at the airport in Israel, they discovered that their luggage had been lost, and the suitcases were never recovered. It was the first and only time their luggage had ever been lost, Vladka later stated. But thankfully, the shofar was safe. Like Moshe, its creator, the shofar was also a survivor.

In 1977, in an emotional ceremony, Moshe Waintreter formally presented the shofar he had shaped and molded in Skarzysko-Kamienna to Israel's foremost Holocaust museum, Yad Vashem, where it remains on permanent exhibit in lasting tribute to the memory of Rabbi Yitzhak Finkler. Although there are many displays in Yad Vashem of various pieces of Judaica that were crafted in the ghettos, the Radoszyce shofar bears the unusual distinction of being the *only* religious ritual artifact to have been made in a concentration camp.

My work is finally done, Moshe thought. Every time people pass the exhibit and read the placard underneath, they will know that there was once a man named Rabbi Yitzhak Finkler, the Grand Rebbe of Radoszyce, who defied the Nazis over and over again.

But the story doesn't end here, nor do most stories end anywhere. Stories have a way of evolving, assuming new incarnations, widening in ever-growing concentric spheres of influence, and undergoing endless permutations until they become different stories altogether. Here is how the story of the Radoszyce shofar developed into a brand-new legend for the second generation:

In 1994, Daniel Wise was a young pulpit rabbi serving at the Desert Synagogue—the first Orthodox synagogue in Palm Springs, California. A minority, Orthodox Jewish residents were loath to advertise their presence in the fabled town. "They just wanted to keep a low profile," Rabbi Wise remembers. "They didn't have a lot of fervor to begin with. . . . In fact, the only two things the congregation had going for it then was the presence of its most illustrious Orthodox member—best-selling author Herman Wouk—and the philanthropy of [Palm Springs resident] singer Frank Sinatra. But in all other respects, it was frustrating to serve as this congregation's rabbi. I was casting about for innovative ways to spark interest in the upcoming High Holiday season, but I couldn't seem to find any exciting idea that might work.

"Just as I was trying to come up with a plan to regenerate the waning religious passions of my membership, I happened to read a story about the unusual shofar that made its home in Yad Vashem. I knew that the one subject that still stirred the hearts and souls of my most disaffected congregants was the Holocaust. What if I could get hold of the Radoszyce shofar and have it blown in our shul? I felt strongly that such an experience would have a deep and powerful impact. It was worth a shot. I picked up the phone and called Dr. Mordecai Paldiel, [former] Director of the Department of the Righteous at Yad Vashem, and one of Israel's foremost Holocaust authorities.

"'I know it would tremendously inspire my congregants to have the Holocaust shofar blown here. What are the chances?' I asked Dr. Paldiel."

Miraculously, Dr. Paldiel's daughter lived near Palm Springs, and he agreed to hand-deliver the shofar when he came to visit her.

"I really wanted to galvanize the Jewish residents of Palm Springs, give them a shot in the arm they wouldn't forget," remembers Rabbi Wise. "So I called a press agent and told her what I planned. I also gave her a brief history of the shofar's creation. On the other end, all I could hear was silence.

"Then she finally said: 'You can't imagine what this story is doing for me. I'm a Polish Catholic, and you're telling me that a Polish Catholic factory foreman helped Moshe Waintreter to craft this shofar. So now I will continue his work and help you tell the story.'

"During Neilah (the last prayer service before Yom Kippur ends), I was shocked to see thousands of people who had come to hear the Holocaust shofar thronging the streets outside the shul. All the major networks and newspapers were there too, with reporters and film crews all over the place. Suddenly, everyone in Palm Springs was Jewish!

"I was asked to blow the shofar, but I didn't dare touch it. To me, it was so holy, I didn't feel worthy. So I gave the honor instead to Larry Pitz, president of our shul. Before he blew the shofar, Larry took about five minutes to compose himself and press his lips against the mouthpiece—he was trembling and crying so much.

"I thought it would be a tiny shofar and would emit only a small sound, but that wasn't the case at all. It was a very respectable-looking shofar and a good size, too, but the big surprise was its sound. Big, beautiful, haunting notes blasted from it, sounding like a million and a half children crying together. Everyone— even the most jaded residents of Palm Springs—was visibly moved, and tears flowed freely. It was indeed a truly memorable moment."

TWELVE YEARS LATER, in 2006, when Rabbi Wise was long gone from Palm Springs, he received a "bolt out of the blue" phone call from a wealthy couple in Palm Springs who had been greatly moved by the story of the Holocaust shofar and decided they wanted to sponsor a movie about it. They were willing to finance the project completely, they said.

"I'll have to obtain permission from Moshe Waintreter," Rabbi Wise said. "Let me call Dr. Paldiel and see if he has his contact information."

But it was an elderly, frail Ida Waintreter who answered the phone when the rabbi called, not Moshe, telling him in quavering tones that Moshe had died of a heart attack when he was seventy-four. "If you want permission, call my son," she directed Rabbi Wise, giving him the phone number of the couple's only child.

The Rebbe's son was affable over the phone, and he instantly gave Rabbi Wise his full-hearted permission. Yet it seemed there was much more to the story.

He told the rabbi that, like many other survivors, his father never spoke of his experiences during the Holocaust . . . until an engagement party changed everything. Someone had proposed a *shidduch* (match) between himself and the daughter of a

Holocaust survivor in Canada. He flew to Canada to meet her, and they could clearly see from the very beginning that they were each other's *bashert* (destined one). After meeting several times, they decided to get engaged. The engagement party was held in Canada, and his father came for the joyous occasion. He started to introduce the two *mechutanim* (fathers-in-law), but instead of warmly greeting each other, as he had expected them to do, they stared at each other in shock and blanched white. Then they began to simultaneously sob and run into each other's arms, whimpering in mingled pain and joy.

Unbeknownst to him, the matchmaker, or anyone else, his future father-in-law turned out to be none other than Shloma, the chassid who had made the borsht for the Radoszyce Rebbe's *arba kosos* for Pesach in 1943!

These two men were the only Radoszyce chassidim who survived Skarzysko-Kamienna—exactly as the Rebbe had promised.

The Radoszyce Rebbe had given Shloma and Moshe his blessing that they would live better years, and indeed they did.

But he had never said a word about making matches for their children.

~ Various sources (see credits, page 256)
and as recounted by Daniel S. Wise to the authors

THE ROSE

red was universally loved in his hometown, where he was a popular guidance counselor at the local high school. Everyone described him as a sweet, caring, and dear person—a "gentle man." But beneath his friendly and kind temperament lurked a troubled soul. Although he was only in his late forties or early fifties (young to me), Fred looked emaciated and much older. He had a debilitating problem that intruded upon the rest of his life and caused tremendous anguish to everyone in his orbit. He couldn't stop drinking alcohol. He hit the booze even harder when it ultimately caused the breakup of his marriage. Despite their father's issues, his daughters lived with Fred most of the time after the divorce.

He was a good friend of mine.

One day, in midst of a conversation, he suddenly turned to me and made me promise that I would take care of his two girls if anything ever happened to him. Fred knew that my husband and I had a penchant for taking in people who touched our hearts and that we had an open house for anyone who needed a place to live. My daughter Ruthie used to laugh that she would never know who would be sleeping in the extra bed in her room when she woke up in the morning! That's how it was in our home. Women fleeing abusive husbands found refuge with us (one man got so mad that we gave his wife shelter that he drove his car into our house, making the front page of the paper!);

homeless people of all sizes, colors, and ages moved in for free; we adopted a troubled teenager, and so on and so forth. I would estimate that over the years, about thirty-five different people lived in our home, some for long stays, others for shorter. Fred knew about our activities, and I suppose he thought we could take care of his daughters if he died prematurely. Which he did.

I don't know who discovered his body, but he was found dead in his apartment. My husband, Howard, was the town's medical examiner, and he determined that Fred had suddenly died of alcohol poisoning. He never had a chance to say good-bye to anyone.

Honoring the promise I made to Fred, I invited his girls to come live with me. It was a temporary arrangement because I knew in time they would eventually go back to their mother. We were just an interim place for them to be until they reestablished their relationship with her. But Fred had asked me to take care of them, and I was determined to keep my pledge.

One day shortly after the girls arrived at my home, we were on our way out to do some errands. As I was closing the front door, I happened to look over by the side of our house. Lo and behold, there was a big beautiful rose growing out of the ground!

This was very strange because there were no rose bushes anywhere on my property. I didn't grow flowers. There had been no rose there the day before, nor had I ever seen one in my yard during the entire eighteen years that I had lived in my house.

You might suggest that some mysterious person came in the middle of the night and planted it there, as a prank or as a gift.

But no . . . that would have been impossible. . . . It was wintertime in northern Michigan, and the ground was hard as a rock—plus there were still several inches of snow on the ground.

This rose was growing directly out of the ground. It was about a foot high. It was the strangest sight I have ever seen. It caused quite a stir in town.

The local newspaper came out to the house to take a picture of the rose, and it made the front page! So I have my verification. Despite how unreal it sounds, this is a true story, photographed and documented for all skeptics to see.

When spring came, however, the rose was gone. . . . And when all the snow had melted and the ground had softened, there was no rose bush where the rose had bloomed . . . and absolutely no clue as to how the rose had gotten to my house in the first place and how it had managed to live during the course of our harsh winter.

How about that!

I always felt that the miraculous rose was Fred saying good-bye to us. I had kept my promise to him—his beloved daughters were safe in my home—and there was only one person I knew who grew roses when he was alive: *Fred*.

~ *Joan Otto*

FAMILY FRIENDS

$\mathcal{D}$ebbie and Sara came from widely divergent geographical and religious backgrounds, but when they both moved to the same street in North Hollywood in the late 1970s, they instantly bonded. Debbie was from Texas and Sara was from Toronto; their background cultures and "mentalities" were exceedingly different, yet they shared a lot of interests and became good friends. They were both young marrieds and undergoing similar experiences at the same time. They often schmoozed about both the joys and the challenges of child-rearing, and one day, just for a little R & R, decided to go shopping. At Loehmann's. (Alas, that discount-store chain—which provided shopping nirvana for droves of bargain-seekers, and where deep friendships sprang from the sheer joy that comes from good-deal hunting—now only exists as an online marketplace.)

But when Debbie and Sara shopped there, Loehmann's was in its heyday. Frenzied shoppers crowded its aisles, and women pounced with glee on fresh merchandise even as it was being unpacked. On a particularly successful foray, Debbie and Sara emerged triumphant from the store; they had fallen in love with the identical skirt, in the same color, and had bought it in their respective sizes. They weren't competitive and didn't feel they had to own an utterly unique item that was different from everyone else's. They were just thrilled that they had found a skirt that fit well and was perfect for their needs.

About a year later they were in front of one of their homes schmoozing when Sara suddenly stopped and said: "Hey, Debbie, I just realized that I haven't seen you wear your skirt for a while. I know you were crazy about it. What happened?"

"Oh, I tore mine," Debbie said regretfully. "It couldn't be fixed. I did *love* that skirt. But now that you mention it, I realize I haven't seen you in your skirt, either. What happened to yours?"

"Wow, this is a coincidence!" Sara exclaimed. "I tore mine, too. How did you tear yours, because I tore mine in such a crazy way you wouldn't believe it."

"I *also* tore my skirt in a crazy way!" Debbie said. "I was going to visit my grandparents' graves in a cemetery, and the fence was locked. There was no caretaker around and no way to get in. Well, I wasn't going to turn around and give up, not after coming such a long way. So I climbed over the fence. The skirt got caught on a fence post and ripped. It's completely ruined, but at least I got to pay my respects to my grandparents."

Sara gaped at Debbie during her recital. "Debbie, you're never going to believe this, but that is exactly how my skirt got torn. *The exact same scenario.* I went to visit my father's grave— which I do every year—and the cemetery was also locked. I also climbed the fence, and the skirt also got torn when I tried to vault over the sharp link chains of the fence."

Goose bumps began to erupt all over Sara's arms.

"Debbie," she asked urgently, "which cemetery did you go to?"

"Oh, it's located in a little town on the East Coast; no one around here would be familiar with it."

"Which little town?" Sara demanded with growing excitement.

"Oh, you probably never heard of it. It's called Vineland, in New Jersey."

"Debbie!" Sarah shrieked. "It's the same cemetery. That's where I tore my skirt, too!"

"But how could this be?" Debbie blinked.

"Come on, Debbie," Sara insisted, "don't you remember that my father's buried there? He owned a chicken farm in Vineland, and we lived there briefly until I was about two. Tragically, he was in a fatal car accident there. Afterward, we moved to Toronto, where I grew up. But you—you come from Dallas—who do you have at the cemetery?"

"My grandparents; they had a chicken farm in Vineland, too!"

"You never told me!"

The two friends stared at each other in disbelief.

"What were the chances?" Sara asks today, a frisson of awe palpable in her voice.

Sara recalled, "The same skirt, the same climb over the fence, the same cemetery. I didn't even know that Debbie had roots in Vineland—I thought she was strictly a Texas girl. It was just wild. We kept reflecting over the strange coincidence and wondered what it meant. It seemed clear that we shared a lot more than just being neighbors . . . but we couldn't quite figure out what it was. We speculated that perhaps my father and Debbie's grandparents knew each other, although they were members of different generations.

"It was a totally weird experience, and what was especially frustrating was that we couldn't tease out the coincidence's meaning or lesson. We were sure that there had to be one, but we couldn't come to any one conclusion. But the coincidence did definitely deepen our connection, emphasizing that our friendship had deeper roots than we originally thought.

"We tried to do some research to see if our families were connected in some way, but so far we haven't been able to unearth a single link. We would love to have some kind of outcome or conclusion to this story, but so far it's still open-ended.

"However, now when I return each year to visit my father's grave in Vineland, I always make sure to stop by Debbie's grandparents' plots in the same cemetery, recite a prayer or two, say hello, and send them regards from their granddaughter—my friend."

~ Sara, as told to the authors

3:38 A.M.

*I*n April 2003, my father-in-law was nearing the end of his life; he'd been suffering from Parkinson's disease for the past seven years, and in the three or four months prior to his death he'd been suffering in a way I'd never seen anyone suffer before.

We live in California, and I was preparing for a trip back east for my father's seventieth birthday party; as my wife later (and sadly) pointed out, "You were celebrating the day of your father's birth while I was preparing for the death of mine." I arrived in New York the night before the party, and went to sleep. The next day, I awoke to a phone call from my wife, informing me that her father had passed away the previous night.

The tears were expected. But what she told me after she wiped them away blew my mind.

The night before, my wife couldn't sleep. She went in to check on our son and daughter, who were eight and five, respectively. My daughter was in her usual splayed-out position on her bed, but my son was curled up in an unusual position. When my wife went into his room to take a closer look, she noticed an expression on his face that he had never made before, awake or asleep, an expression in which his eyes were tightly shut and his lips were pursed up, almost like a duck's.

It was the *exact* expression my father-in-law made on a regular basis, more out of habit than anything else, but one we all very much associated with him.

My wife glanced at the clock; it was 3:38 a.m.

The next morning, the hospital, which was about forty miles away from our house, called to let her know that he had passed that night.

At 3:38 a.m.

My son has never made that expression again since then. And as a postscript, my wife found herself waking up at 3:38 a.m. every night for several weeks after that. While that situation might very well be explained away by an unconsciously recalibrated body clock, my son's expression, which coincided with the very moment of my father-in-law's passing, made me a believer in some form of consciousness after the passing of the body. It was simply too uncanny . . . simply too miraculous to be a complete coincidence.

~ *David Kukoff*

A TIME TO DANCE

*A*nyone suffering from the tribulations that infertility can bring will fully resonate with the pain of another childless person who longs for a child: this pain is universal and knows no bounds. But exactly how this pain is expressed may be altogether different, specific to the culture and context in which the childless person resides. In the greater secular culture, where people speak freely of their difficulties and all kinds of self-help groups proliferate, infertility is discussed openly and carries no shame. But for ultra-Orthodox Jews, for whom family is the defining core of their lives, a world without children is one of the greatest scourges with which they can be smitten. Compounding this sense of failure and emptiness is the culture of privacy in which they dwell. People in ultra-Orthodox enclaves don't speak as freely as their counterparts do in "the outside world." They suffer their pains in private. And consequently, they often have no one to reach out to for help.

In 1993, Rabbi Shaul Rosen and his wife, Brany Rosen, who had suffered from infertility for many years before finally knowing the joy of parenthood, decided to bring "the problem" out into the open and help other struggling couples. They began to offer a variety of free medical referral and social services to assist childless couples, and their organization, which they named A TIME, flourished, expanding from beyond their home to a suite of modern offices staffed by multiple employees. The need was and continues to be great—far greater than they had originally envisioned—and consequently A TIME evolved into a worldwide organization with branches in the United States, Israel, England, and Canada. The Rosens' dedication to the cause was passionate and constant. Their reputation in the ultra-Orthodox community grew along with their organization, and this reputation is impeccable. They are highly regarded for their integrity. Although A TIME was based in New York, petitioners flowed to their offices from all over the world.

In 2001, the Rosens and their partners—Rabbi Naftali Weiss and his wife, Yocheved Weiss (of blessed memory)—flew to Israel to launch a satellite operation for the childless people of Israel who clamored for help in their country, too. Four years later they organized a retreat in Tiberias (near the Sea of Galilee) for forty-five Israeli couples suffering from infertility. They all spent the weekend together in a hotel, where they convened for workshops, discussions, and a little R & R, too. Infertility exacts a heavy toll, and a little recreation and socializing provided some balm for the couples' scarred spirits.

Tiberias is just a few miles from the legendary town of Meron, where the gravesite of the renowned first-century sage Rabbi Shimon bar Yochai is located. Rabbi Shimon is best known as the author of the Zohar, a book of mystical revelations, and over the millennia religious Jews have come to view his gravesite as a place where prayers could be heard and miracles performed. Multitudes from all over the world still make personal pilgrimages to his grave to pray for children or to appeal for healing of other physical and emotional problems.

Consequently, it was only natural that, given the retreat's proximity to Meron, the itinerary for the A TIME participants included a trip to Rabbi Shimon bar Yochai's gravesite; they planned to visit the gravesite on Saturday night and to pray there as well. But when they arrived, they found, to their dismay, that it was thronged with tourists. The workshop participants—who felt self-conscious about their status as an assembly of childless couples—weren't completely comfortable praying for children in front of their religious cohorts (some of whom they knew); they were unwilling to be pointed at and pitied.

Someone suggested that the group pray instead at the gravesite of Rabbi Shimon bar Yochai's son, Elazar, located just behind Rabbi Shimon's grave. Elazar was a saintly person in his own right; he had steadfastly stayed at his father's side in a cave for twelve years while Rabbi Shimon hid from the Romans, subsisting on carobs and water while studying holy texts. The men in the group agreed that the area surrounding Rabbi Elazar's tomb was infinitely quieter and better suited for their purposes. They formed a circle and began to sing and dance. Still choosing to remain discreet, they deliberately avoided any overt references to childbearing in their public prayers and lusty songs.

As the men danced, a dark-skinned man wearing a short blue jacket and cap approached the circle, as if he wanted to join them. He separated the hands of two men to break into the circle, kissing their hands as he did so. After a few turns he began singing a spirited song containing the words *zerach chaya v'kayam* (in Hebrew, "offspring live and endure").

The men were embarrassed by the stranger's allusion to children—how did he know? They didn't want their childless status revealed to the throngs nearby. Meanwhile, the man continued to dance with greater and greater fervor, breaking away into the middle of the circle, attempting to pull men out into his orbit, one by one, to dance with him. Most of the men resisted—the stranger's odd behavior was off-putting—but eventually the stranger did manage to pull four of the men into the circle to dance with him. At the conclusion of each dance, the stranger kissed his dancing partner on the forehead. When the dance ended, he smiled at the group and disappeared as mysteriously as he had arrived. They stared after his retreating figure, perplexed and agape.

Rabbi Rosen turned to Rabbi Weiss. "Don't you think there's something very strange about all of this?" he asked. "What just happened seems very odd to me. Where did this man come from? How did he know that most of us were childless? You know what I'm going to do? I'm going to write down the names of the four people the stranger danced with so I don't forget." Later, back at the hotel, Rabbi Rosen pulled up his files and matched the names to their medical cases. Two of the cases were extremely hard; for years doctors had tried all the interventions they could possibly perform, and failed. They were doubtful that additional medicine, surgeries, or procedures would ever help.

The next day, the group of Israeli participants returned home, and Rabbi Rosen and Rabbi Weiss went out to tour a local *shuk* (outdoor market). They were walking near a booth that was hung with pictures of Jewish sages and saints, and one of them bore an inscription proclaiming it was a picture of Rabbi Shimon bar Yochai. Rabbi Rosen turned to Rabbi Weiss and said, "I don't know if that is Rabbi Shimon bar Yochai, but it sure looks like the man we danced with last night."

Several days after the strange episode, the Rosens and the Weisses returned to the United States and got swept up in daily life: busy with their families, their jobs, and their work for A TIME. A few months later, they received a phone call from one of the couples whose husband had danced with the stranger in Meron. "We're pregnant!" they said joyfully.

One by one, *all* of the couples whose husbands had danced with the dark-skinned man in Meron called with the same happy news. All four couples had their yearning for a child finally fulfilled and experienced the unbridled joy of welcoming four healthy babies into the world.

And some of them were even given the name Shimon, in honor of the miracle that occurred in Meron.

To this day, everyone still wonders: Who *was* that man?

Rabbi Shaul Rosen and Brany Rosen are telling their story today to emphasize the unfathomable power of prayer for those desperately seeking miracles. They want to impart hope to the hopeless and share their experience as a vivid testament to what prayer can achieve. They also want people to become more aware of how little we know who anyone really is, who is holy and who is not, and how everyone should be treated with respect.

When the four men embraced a stranger and danced with him in order to give him honor—just because he was human—incredible miracles did indeed occur. And one of those miracles happened to the Rosens themselves, as Rabbi Rosen was among the men who did not wish to shame the stranger by refusing his invitation to dance. Nine months later, a different kind of music resounded in the Rosen home—the joyous wailing of a newborn infant. "Long before this experience, we had thankfully overcome our infertility and already had five children. It had been six years since we had last had a child—a stillborn—and we didn't think we would ever have another child," Brany Rosen remarks. "So when I became pregnant again, I was shocked. But my husband had also danced with the holy stranger, so we too were blessed."

~ Rabbi Shaul Rosen and Brany Rosen,
as told to the authors

THE LONG CAB RIDE

*I*t was the late 1970s, and Leslie Westreich had finished three grueling years of law school and a bar exam. He was now going to embark on his first vacation from a law firm where he was newly employed. He couldn't wait to get away for a bit. He decided to celebrate by taking a trip to Europe.

But family loyalty imposed a slight change to his itinerary. Before touring the Continent, he resolved to make a stop in Israel, where his grandfather, who had passed away the previous year, was buried, to pay his respects.

In 1938 his grandparents, with their four daughters, had fled Berlin, the capital of Nazi Germany, and immigrated to America. After the Six-Day War, with all of their children married and settled, they had finally fulfilled their lifelong dream to move from America to the Holy Land. It was in this land where they wanted to live, and ultimately, it was where they wanted to be buried. After his grandfather's passing, his grandmother moved to New York to be with her daughters, but Leslie's family had held on to their apartment in Jerusalem, so he had a place to stay.

Leslie was told by his mother that his grandfather was buried in a city called Beit Shemesh in a new Ashkenazi cemetery. Leslie's mother said that the cemetery was so new that there were really no section markers, but that he'd find the gravestone because it was one of the few graves located beneath a tree.

Once in Israel, Leslie didn't anticipate having any trouble finding the grave. He tried taking a cab to Beit Shemesh, but the cabdriver took him to an ancient Sephardic cemetery and insisted that there was no other cemetery in the city. There was no arguing with the cabbie; the trip was futile and Leslie returned to Jerusalem.

The next day, Leslie got into another cab and made the long trip yet again. This time he was careful and located a cabbie who knew the location of the new Ashkenazic cemetery in Beit Shemesh. When Leslie arrived he began walking through the cemetery, looking for a tombstone located beneath a tree, the only clue he had as to the whereabouts of the grave.

It was a torrid August day, and the Middle Eastern sun beat mercilessly on Leslie's head. The few graves at the new cemetery were quite spread out. Despite the conditions, Leslie walked from one gravesite to another, reading the headstones. He was extremely thirsty and hot, and becoming more and more exhausted as time passed. He just couldn't find the grave.

The driver was waiting impatiently for him. With the sweat rolling down his face and his heart heavy with disappointment, Leslie felt he had no choice but to give up the search. He got back in the cab and returned to his grandparents' apartment at 30 Jabotinsky Street in Jerusalem.

The following day, he decided not to repeat the previous two days' trying experience. Instead, he thought he'd go to Kever Rachel, the gravesite of the biblical matriarch Rachel, a site Jews often visit to pour out their hearts and pray. The tomb had a small, dome-shaped structure built over it, sheltering visitors from the sun. Leslie figured he'd go, he'd pray, and he'd keep his grandfather's soul in mind as if he'd gone to visit his grave.

He hailed a cab and asked the driver how much he'd charge to take him to Kever Rachel. The driver, a coarse-looking fellow in jeans, named a price in lirot (the Israeli currency at that time) that was the equivalent of about $75 (a huge sum in the 1970s)— to travel to a site that isn't much more than twenty minutes from Jerusalem.

"Are you crazy?" Leslie retorted. "That's outrageous!"

The two men haggled furiously. Finally the driver said, "Okay, I'll take you for twenty-five dollars. But you can only stay inside for ten minutes!"

Leslie shrugged, not quite taking him seriously. They set off for Kever Rachel and arrived without incident. Once there, Leslie went inside and began to pray. The holy ambience of the site uplifted him, made him feel transported to a loftier sphere; he read the words in his prayer book and drank in new depths of meaning. He thought of his grandfather, and prayed for him. Ten minutes passed. Leslie lost all sense of time and at least ten more minutes passed again.

When he finally emerged out into the blinding Middle Eastern sunlight, his soul uplifted, he was jolted back to reality when he found himself face-to-face with a fuming cabdriver. "We said only ten minutes!" the cabbie snarled as he headed onto the main road to Jerusalem. "Now the price is going to be fifty dollars!"

The two did not exchange another word. Leslie couldn't wait to get home and out of this cab; *this driver was really a piece of work*, he thought: *absolutely obnoxious.*

As they neared Jerusalem city proper, the disgruntled cabbie broke the silence and asked, "Where to?"

"30 Jabotinsky Street," Leslie said.

As they continued on, the cabbie remarked, "Saba and Savta [endearing names in Hebrew for 'grandfather' and 'grandmother'] lived there."

Although curious about the coincidence, Leslie did not want to get into another exchange with the cabbie. He sat in silence and thought, *Does this guy really think I care where his grandparents lived?*

After a few more minutes, the cabbie asked Leslie again, "On which floor do you live?"

"The second floor," Leslie answered.

"Saba and Savta lived there," the driver responded almost immediately.

Leslie wrinkled his brow. He knew there were only two apartments on the second floor. One belonged to his grandparents, and the other belonged to Daisy, a very old lady Leslie thought must have been close to one hundred years old. Could this cabbie have such an old grandmother?

"Saba and Savta's name was Gewirtz," the cabbie was now saying.

Leslie almost fainted. *His* grandparents' name was Gewirtz! How could this cabdriver possibly be related to him? "You couldn't be a grandson of Gewirtz!" he choked out.

The cabbie smiled. "Well, as you see, I'm a driver," he said. "Back in 1969, I was driving at the airport, and my next fare was this sweet elderly couple with a bunch of suitcases who had just arrived in Israel and who told me that they were making Aliyah [the act of Jewish immigration to Israel]. They informed me that they would be going to 30 Jabotinsky Street, their new apartment in Jerusalem.

"On the road to Jerusalem, the old man was telling me with great emotion how he was finally realizing his dream to live in Israel. He'd survived the Holocaust, made a home and raised a family in America, but had always wanted to come to live here.

"I felt so inspired by this elderly man, and his tremendous love for the Holy Land. The entire ride to Jerusalem to their new home, your grandparents were so overcome with joy and gratitude. By the time we arrived at 30 Jabotinsky Street, I was overcome with feeling for this couple.

"When we arrived at the destination, I unloaded the car. I looked at all the suitcases, I looked at them, and I couldn't just let them schlep the luggage up the stairs by themselves. I brought everything upstairs for them. When they opened the front door, I noticed that while all their furniture had arrived, it was still sitting in boxes. I thought, *How can I leave them alone in this situation? They couldn't possibly assemble it all on their own*. The next day was already Friday, right before the Sabbath. I spent the rest of the afternoon helping them set up their apartment.

"It was a big job, and when I finished, I asked them to just pay for the agreed taxi fare from the airport to Jerusalem. Your grandmother said, 'First, you come to me tomorrow (Erev Shabbat) for some chicken soup. After that, I'll pay you your fare.' The next day I returned. She served me chicken soup and paid me my fare. We became rather close afterward, and

I became their personal driver wherever they went and always called them *saba v'savta* [grandfather and grandmother]."

Leslie sat in the back seat, astonished. It didn't surprise him that his openhearted grandparents had befriended an Israeli man so different from themselves, but what were the odds he would end up in this same man's taxi? Leslie let the thought settle in, then he looked at this cabbie with a whole new set of eyes and asked: "So maybe you know where my grandfather is buried?"

The man gave a snort. "Do *I* know where he is buried? Do *I* know?" He opened the glove compartment and took out a well-thumbed Book of Psalms and a yarmulke. He handed the prayer book to Leslie. He opened the front cover and showed Leslie the inside flap.

"Do you recognize this name?" he asked.

"Of course I do," said Leslie, utterly shocked. "That's the name of my aunt."

"Exactly," said the cabbie. "Your aunt came to Israel, and she gave me one hundred dollars and made me promise that I would go on a regular basis to your grandfather's gravesite to pray on behalf of the family. And I do."

The elderly couple's personal chauffeur then proceeded to personally chauffeur their grandson to the gravesite he'd made a special trip to visit, and they prayed together at Saba's gravesite.

~*Leslie Westreich, as told to the authors*

ᔇᓍᓂ

JUST FIVE MORE MINUTES

About seven months after my father died, my niece gave birth to a baby boy, who would be named after my father. There was a lot of talk in the family about what a blessing it was for my father's spirit, how we'd have someone to carry on my father's name, how we prayed that the baby would manifest all my father's good character traits . . . and, of course, since he was a firstborn son, how we'd have an opportunity to have a *pidyon haben* (a Jewish ritual associated with the birth of a firstborn son).

But I was only half listening to the conversations. My only thought, which kept reverberating through my mind, was that when this baby has his bris and gets a name, my father will truly be gone. This will be part of the closure that everyone keeps going on about. I will no longer be able to pretend that he has just gone on a trip, and is coming back soon. It was the real deal.

I walked around that week, hearing the tantrums in my head that this innocent little boy had provoked in me. No, no, I don't want to go to the bris. I don't care how cute this baby is. I want my father. . . . I want him back. Give me just five more minutes with my father! I was embarrassed to share my feelings with anyone in my family. After all, shouldn't I be happy that the baby would carry my father's name? Shouldn't I be happy about becoming an aunt all over again? (And I am a really *great* aunt.) I didn't think anyone would understand my feelings, so I didn't share them. And so the crying jags began. Grief and loss, combined with the finality of it all.

Crying as I stood at the sink washing dishes.

Crying as I did the laundry.

Crying as I cooked, producing salty, watery meals.

Crying as I sat on the subway with my newspaper.

Crying as I pulled out my cell phone to order a ticket to a major *chazanut* (Jewish liturgical singing) concert for my father because he loved them.

Crying again when I remembered what had happened.

The bris was getting closer, the crying was getting worse, and I could find no way to calm myself. All I kept thinking was . . . what I wouldn't do for just five more minutes with my father.

Two nights before the bris, my father appeared to me in a dream. I'm not sure what I expected, but there were no wings, no halo, and certainly no aura around him. He looked . . . like himself.

He wore his houndstooth wool coat, his hat, and his everyday shoes. It might have been just an ordinary business day, except that it wasn't, and I knew that even in my dream.

"Totty!" I rushed forward and hugged him. I felt his warmth.

"Mamala," he said, "I'm here only for a short while. You want to go for a drive?" I did.

We climbed into his Avalon. In the passenger seat, I just kept hugging myself with excitement. I actually got to spend time with Totty . . . alone!

My father was never much of a talker, so I chatted the entire time, like a five-year-old on speed.

"How is it up there, Totty? Are you happy? Do you miss us? Oy, Totty, we miss you so badly. Is it true that you are near the Kisei HaKavod [Throne of Glory]? You know about the baby, right?" and on and on and on . . . so that I barely noticed when he disappeared, and I woke up.

I didn't really need answers to my questions. Yes, he looked happy, and his heartfelt hug told me how much he missed us. Of course, he knew about the baby. How could he not? He was booked on the same "flight" as Eliyahu Hanavi [Elijah the Prophet] to arrive at the bris.

I woke up that morning with a special kind of contentment. As I went about my day with a song in my heart and a spring in my step, I was full of gratitude to my father for fulfilling my wishes, and thought the "trip" must have been a long and arduous one.

The morning of the bris dawned, and I was ready—physically, emotionally, and spiritually. My prayers that morning were filled with a depth that I have rarely experienced since. As the grandfather announced the name of the baby, everyone in the family was crying. Not me. A kind of peace settled over me. My father was gone, but not really gone. There will be great-grandchildren to keep his memory and legacy alive.

And I am still his (favorite?) daughter, and he is still my devoted father. Look how he came down from the heavens to grant my request for just five more minutes with him.

~ *Chaya Sarah Stark*

JIMMY

Three generations of Sanchezes had yielded no male progeny, so when a baby boy was finally born to Alina, her grandparents rejoiced.

"There was nothing they wouldn't or couldn't do for Jimmy," Alina Sanchez Fenton remembers nostalgically. "They basically lived for him. He was pampered, humored, indulged. They babysat constantly and visited often. Their love for him was endless."

But when Jimmy was only two, his great-grandfather died, so it was with his great-grandmother Magda (whom he called Aba) that he forged his deepest bond.

Magda was old in years but young in spirit. She was a typical great-grandmother in that she was loving, kind, and warm and baked delicious homemade cookies. She was atypical by virtue of the fact that it was also she who taught Jimmy how to climb a fence, ride a bike, and slide a scooter across the street. Everyone marveled at their kinship and affinity. Even as Jimmy got older and his contemporaries began to lose interest in their grandparents, his profound love for his great-grandmother endured.

In 1994, when Jimmy was only twenty-two, he was gunned down in a senseless street mugging. He was shot in the heart by a nineteen-year-old who wanted his watch.

Alina didn't know how to tell her grandmother that Jimmy was dead.

"I thought she would just crumble, but in the end it was she who supported me, not the other way around. She was very much there for me. I couldn't have continued without her help."

Five years later, in 1999, Magda Sanchez died at the age of ninety-five.

"She had a full life, and of course we were very grateful for all the years we had together, but still, how could we not be sad? We had lost our dear Aba, and we were in a lot of pain."

The night before the funeral, family and friends gathered at the funeral parlor for the viewing. The chapel contained several rooms, and when it was time to leave, Alina used the key the chapel director had given her to lock the room that contained Magda's coffin.

It was then that she first noticed the guest book near the door that visitors are asked to sign before entering a room to pay their respects.

"What should we do with the guest book?" Alina's mother worried.

"Let's just leave it here, and we'll take it home tomorrow when the funeral is over, OK?" Alina replied.

"Are you sure it's all right?" her mother fretted. "Maybe we should take it home for the night."

Her mother's concern prompted Alina to glance casually at the guest book and scan the names that had been scribbled into its pages.

"I had never bothered looking at a guest book before," Alina recalls, "but something just made me take a look. Maybe it was my mother's near obsession with it. Anyway, I noticed that the very last signature in the book belonged to my engaged daughter's future mother-in-law, R———. Then I turned off the lights, locked the door, and closed up for the night."

The next day, the family returned to the funeral home to gather for the procession to the church where the mass would take place. "I was the first to arrive at the funeral parlor," Alina remembers vividly, "the only one with the key to our room. As I entered, I noticed my mother's friend waiting outside for us to open the door. I greeted her, unlocked the door, and headed straight for the guest book."

In retrospect, Alina remains puzzled by her own action.

"I wasn't in the habit of perusing guest books," she insists again. "They never interested me in the slightest." But because her mother had seemed so anxious about the guest book the night before, something drew her to the stand on which it was placed, to check to see that the pages were still intact.

It was then that she saw the entry.

JIMMY FENTON, with a little cross next to it (indicating deceased), was written in a childish scrawl, right below R———'s signature, the last name entered into the book before Alina had closed up the night before.

"The handwriting was not that of an adult," Alina says, "but clearly one belonging to a young child. It reminded me of the peculiar way Jimmy used to sign his name when he was in grade school." Staring in disbelief at the signature, Alina thought she would faint. Trembling, she turned toward the woman who had entered the chapel with her. "Was there anyone near or outside the chapel when you got here?" Alina demanded.

"No," the woman answered, bewildered by Alina's intensity.

"Did you notice this signature in the book?" Alina asked, pointing to Jimmy's entry.

"Yes, I did," the woman said, "which is why I entered my name two lines underneath."

"And you didn't see anyone hanging around here earlier?" Alina pressed.

"Absolutely not. What's going on?"

When Alina's daughter and husband arrived a few minutes later, she pounced on them in a frenzied state, insisting that they tell her if either one of them had entered Jimmy's name in the guest book.

They looked at her in shock. "Why would we ever do such a thing?" they gasped.

No one could understand who or why would pull a prank like that. Or was it a prank?

When Alina returned from the cemetery that day with the guest book in hand, she hunted for a scrapbook she had helped Magda compile during the last days of her life—a scrapbook that contained old photographs, tattered mementos, ancient mail. It also included, Alina remembered, an old Valentine's Day card from Jimmy to his beloved Aba. He had given it to his great-grandmother when he was only eight years old.

When Alina found the little Valentine's Day card tucked into the scrapbook, she opened it and studied the handwriting. Then she spread open the guest book to the page that contained Jimmy's entry.

The handwriting was exactly the same.

"Jimmy always had a very distinctive way of writing his name," Alina says. "It wasn't similar to other childish scrawls, but was very idiosyncratic and unique. It wasn't a handwriting that you could easily confuse with someone else's."

Studying the evidence before her very eyes, Alina could only come up with one conclusion: Jimmy had loved his great-grandmother so much that he had come to pay his respects at her funeral. And he loved his family so much that he had come to be with them to share their grief.

Alina interprets the baffling incident this way: "We felt that we had been given a sign from above, reassurance from Jimmy, that in some way he was still with us, and that one day we would all be together again."

~ Alina S. Fenton

THE BIRTHDAY CALL

In March 1989, my mother died of cancer following surgery to remove a tumor. We hadn't even known she had cancer until the surgery, and then she died eleven days later. It was a shock to all of us.

On June 23, 1990, on what would have been her seventy-third birthday, I was alone in my house, getting ready to go out for the evening. My husband was out back doing yard work. Since it was summer, all the windows were open. I was startled by the sound of a phone being dialed, broadcast as if it was on speakerphone. I heard the tones as each number was pressed.

The first time I heard the noise, I barely paid attention. Then the phone was dialed a second time, and I thought, *How very odd that I can hear my neighbors dialing their phones. All these years—even in summertime when the windows are wide open—I've never been able to hear them dial their phones before.* But when I heard the phone being dialed a third time, I was spooked. I realized that the clear and unmistakable sounds of buttons being punched out on a touch-tone speakerphone were not coming from my neighbor's house at all, but rather, mysteriously, from mine.

This is weird, I thought. I looked out the window to check on my husband and saw him still stationed in the yard, diligently weeding away. No one else is in the house but me. Who could be using the phone? I headed toward my husband's empty office—the source of those shrill speakerphone noises—and saw that the red light on his phone was on. It lit up whenever it was in use.

I picked up the phone, and the voice of my father came on the line, asking with sharp annoyance, "Who are you? Why do you keep calling me and not saying anything?"

Totally perplexed, I said, "Daddy, what are you doing on my phone?"

"What do you mean, what am I doing on your phone?" he bellowed. "What are *you* doing? Are you calling me or what?"

"Daddy!" I shouted in exasperation. "I didn't call you. Didn't you call me?"

It was then that I realized that my phone had been dialing his number—not once, not twice, but three separate times. My father's phone number was not on speed dial, since this was my husband's business phone, and he did not have my father's number programmed on it. As much as I would have liked to, I could not chalk up the incident to a phone glitch or an operating malfunction. And there was not a single other soul in the house at the time.

Who had made that call?

Both my father and I reached the same conclusion at the same time. The anonymous dialer could be one person and one person only—my mom.

After I hung up the phone, I went back to my bedroom and picked up the framed photograph I keep near my bed. I addressed the photo.

"OK, Mother," I laughed, "I'm sorry I didn't wish you a happy birthday before."

I'm convinced that the "mysterious caller" kept persistently dialing until I went to investigate. Once I wished my mother "Happy Birthday" out loud, the dialing abruptly stopped, and the mysterious "glitch" never occurred again.

~ *Janet White Sperber*

MEDICAL SCHOOL MIRACLE

From childhood on, Nathan Stein always dreamed about becoming a doctor, but it was a dream that he initially had to defer and later completely abandon.

When Nathan was only one year into college, the Great Depression imposed its stark reality upon his family, as it did upon countless millions. Forced to quit school and get a job to help support his parents and siblings, Nathan saw his dreams slowly dwindle away. *Maybe one day a child of mine, or at the very least a child of theirs, will be able to become the doctor I never could be*, he sighed with regret.

Decades later, Nathan began to pin his hopes on his grandson, Kevin Ladin, with whom he had an especially warm relationship. "Kevin," he would repeat over and over again, "I hope you'll become the doctor I always wanted to be." Sadly, when Kevin was only nine years old, Nathan Stein died. But the dreams he had so passionately implanted in Kevin lived on.

For Kevin, like his grandfather, committed himself at a young age to pursuing the goal Nathan Stein had never been able to achieve. He ardently wanted to become a physician and heal the sick. And, as time passed, the dream became more entrenched in his mind, being, and soul.

But where to find the money for medical school?

When at age twenty three, Kevin was a senior at Pennsylvania State University, he began to apply to various medical schools with a high level of anxiety. How would he pay for the first year's tuition of fifteen thousand dollars? His parents both worked as real estate brokers, and they stepped up their efforts to bring in more business.

One day, his father, Sherman Ladin, noticed an ad in a local paper placed by an owner trying to sell his own residence.

"Normally, I don't call people who advertise on their own," Sherman later told the *Philadelphia Inquirer*. But, as he explained to the newspaper, he was suddenly seized by an uncontrollable urge to call the number, an urge he couldn't quite explain. It was uncharacteristic of him to pursue business in this matter.

The owners weren't very receptive to his "cold" call, either. They wanted to sell the house themselves and forego a broker's commission. They told Sherman they would wait several days to see what kind of response they got to their ad. If they couldn't sell the house on their own, they'd eventually call him back, they promised.

And they kept their word.

The owners arranged for Sherman to come see the house on a Tuesday. The appointment was formally set, and Sherman penciled it into his calendar. But when he told his wife, she exclaimed with surprise: "What? Did you forget that we're going to Atlantic City on Tuesday? You have to change the appointment!"

Sherman called the homeowners, and a new appointment was rescheduled for Monday afternoon at 3 p.m. "Three o'clock it is, then!" he confirmed. But later that day, the homeowners called him and said that now they had to change the time. The third—and final—appointment was scheduled for Monday morning at 11 a.m.

When Sherman approached the house, whose address the owners had given him over the phone, he experienced a minor shock. "When I walked up to the front door, I realized that this was the house my in-laws had lived in fifteen years earlier, and it was a very strange feeling," he recalled.

As the T——s, the current owners of the house, ushered him into the living room, he began to tell them about the strange coincidence. But he barely had a chance to say a few words when the doorbell rang.

"No, I'm so sorry, but there's some mistake," he heard the T——s tell the mail carrier at the door, who was holding a certified letter in his hand. "There's no one here by that name. We never heard of a Nathan Stein . . ."

Sherman Ladin jumped up from his chair. "Hey, that was *my father-in-law*!" he exclaimed.

Telling the mail carrier that his father-in-law had died fourteen years ago, he offered to sign for the registered letter, which just happened to be from a bank.

It was a notice about a dormant account that had never been claimed. A dormant account of Nathan Stein's that *no one*—not his wife, nor his daughter or son-in-law—knew anything about. An account that would be forfeited to the state if it were not claimed soon. An account that contained . . . fifteen thousand dollars: the exact amount that Kevin needed for his medical school tuition.

"I am sure that my father wanted my husband to be in his old house at the same time that the mailman came with the registered letter," Shirley Ladin, Nathan's daughter, told reporters. "It had to be that way. Can you think of any other reason for that happening?"

Her husband agreed.

"I was put in that house at precisely that time to make sure Kevin would get the money for his first year's medical school tuition," Sherman Ladin said.

"My father was always there to make things right for us, and he's still doing it," Shirley Ladin said. "There's no doubt in my mind that my father made this happen and that he's watching us to this day."

~ Yitta Halberstam, courtesy of Sherman Ladin

THE BIGGEST ROSE

*T*had watched roses blooming outside my kitchen window for fifteen years. I loved those magnificent beauties, but I never cut them to bring them indoors. Strange as it may seem, they lived only a few days each season before the petals began falling to the ground and the flowers disappeared.

One summer, we had a drought and my beautiful flowers did not bloom at all. In addition, I had neglected to water them because I was consumed with sadness. My beloved mother—my friend, my teacher, my confidante—had been terminally ill for months, and I was heartbroken and helpless. Finally, one scorching day in June, the inevitable happened: my dear mother died.

On the day of the funeral, the ground was parched as the temperature soared to 100 degrees. When I returned home, I was greeted outside my kitchen window by the biggest, most magnificent red rose I had ever seen. Not only was it exquisite, but it was also huge! Such a perfect specimen could never have grown to such greatness unnoticed. I am positive now, as I was then, that the rose did not exist before my mother's funeral. It appeared, as if by magic, just after my mother was laid to rest.

All who came to pay their respects during that week after my mother's death marveled at the size and beauty of the rose. I looked out my window every morning expecting to see red petals on the ground, but the rose remained intact. Not one petal fell from it during that week or the next, or even during the entire month after my mother's death.

On one of those hot, dry, windless days, as my son, my daughter, and I sat outside on the patio, the rose and its branch began to wave wildly before our very eyes. We immediately realized that no other branches were moving; no blades of grass were stirring. We were all in awe—afraid to breathe for fear of erasing the enchanting scene. And then one of my children quietly said: "I think Gram is telling us something. Let's try to understand."

When I described the incident to a friend who is a rabbi, he immediately explained that miracles happen to us every day—that God often sends us messages through nature—but that we must be open to receive them. He told me very matter-of-factly: "Of course, that rose is a messenger from your mother. She's telling you not to worry because she's doing fine now in a place of beauty and greatness."

And so it was that the rose continued to live and shed beauty and generate memories. When it was finally time for it to depart, after eight comforting months, the petals did not fall one by one. The rose slowly shriveled up, turned black, and remained completely intact. There it stayed until my gardener trimmed the rosebush and cut it off. I had forgotten to tell him the story of my beloved mother and the special message she had sent in that miraculous rose. I often ponder what would have happened to that rose had my gardener let nature take its course.

~ *Gail Raab*

THE MATCHMAKER

When single mom Naomi Schur* first traveled to Israel in 1978 with her nine-year-old son, Jason, she had two overriding goals: to provide her child with a Jewish education, and to become Jewishly literate herself. She achieved those objectives by placing Jason in a Jerusalem-based school while she enrolled in a yeshiva for "returnees to Judaism." Mother and son both adapted well to their new environments; instead of experiencing culture shock, they felt they'd returned "home."

Naomi's transition at the yeshiva was facilitated by the warm welcome she received there. She was embraced with kindness and acceptance by both her classmates and her instructors. But of all the teachers at the school, there was one outstanding rabbi who took particular pains to help integrate the Schurs, bringing them home to his wife and family for Shabbat often. "We spent a lot of time at the Levinson home," Naomi reminisces. "They lived an American lifestyle, which was familiar to us, and we hit it off. One of their sons was Jason's age, and they became close. We truly felt part of the family. Ruth, the rabbi's wife, was a fantastic human being, and she and I were devoted friends."

Six years later, Naomi and Jason returned to Boston, where she resumed her original career teaching at the college level, and Jason continued his Jewish studies at Maimonides School.

"I left Israel on May 17, 1984," Naomi recalled when we talked, "exactly thirty years, two months, and twelve days ago."

*All names in this story are pseudonyms.

To her, the Holy Land was home, and life in Boston was a self-imposed exile. She counted every day that she was gone.

Sadly, the Schurs and the Levinsons lost touch, and in 2000 someone told Naomi that Ruth had died of breast cancer. Naomi felt a pang that their ties had loosened over the years and that she had not been with Ruth in her time of need. But before she could even write a condolence card to Rabbi Levinson, someone else told her that he had already remarried. Apparently, before her death, Ruth had articulated her concern that her husband would not be able to cope alone, and she had *insisted* that he find another suitable spouse as soon as possible. A few months later, he did. Naomi now felt it was inappropriate to express her sympathies, so she refrained from contacting him.

But on the night of May 22, 2014, Ruth suddenly appeared to Naomi in a dream. "Naomi," she said firmly, "you've really been out of touch. You have to keep in touch."

In the dream, Naomi responded, "Not to sound rude, but you've already crossed over, and your husband is a *man*. It wouldn't be modest for me to reach out to him." Ruth agreed. "You're right on both counts," she said, "but still you have to get in touch . . . even though he's a man." Then she faded away.

Naomi vividly remembers the date of the dream, May 22, because the date was important to her. It was the *yahrtzeit* of her father's death, which she punctiliously observed.

Naomi initially disregarded Ruth's message, but eventually she felt compelled to follow her friend's "orders." She found Rabbi Levinson's e-mail address on the yeshiva website, and she sent him a picture of her son and the rest of her family dressed in religious garb to give him the *nachas* (joy and satisfaction) that his investment in her family had not been in vain, and that they'd remained observant all these years. The rabbi responded with a gracious e-mail, thanking Naomi for the photo, and then mentioned that he was recovering from a terrible car accident. Far worse, his second wife had died from the injuries she had sustained in the same accident, and he was in mourning.

Naomi felt terrible and wrote him back. Soon, their e-mails began accelerating to several a day. Then they began speaking on the phone. "All this time, I prayed that God would send the rabbi someone to take care of him. 'He's so alone,' I cried. 'You have to send him his *bashert* (destined one).' But I never thought it would be *me*."

One day on the phone, Rabbi Levinson proposed. "I was shocked. I didn't think I was wife material. . . . I was a college professor in my sixties with a great income. I never thought I'd marry again. But apparently Ruth was busy in Heaven, running the show and still watching over her husband as faithfully as she had on this earthly plane. I knew this had to be true because I later learned that the car accident occurred on the *exact same date and at the same time* as my dream in which Ruth appeared."

~ *Anonymous, as told to the authors*

THE MEMENTO BOX

Several years ago, Diana was a high-powered newswoman reporting on medical news for a Miami affiliate. Because of her public exposure and the expertise she demonstrated on TV, she was constantly receiving requests from viewers, who asked her for many different forms of help. As much as she would have liked to, she knew it was impossible to respond to them all. If she had, her life would have simply spun out of control.

But one day, she got a request from a viewer that touched her heart. Mary L——'s husband, Carl, had contracted a rare form of cancerous tumor called a liposarcoma in his upper thigh. His doctor had told him that the only way to eliminate this type of cancer was to amputate the leg. Mary didn't know Diana personally, but she contacted her in desperation, hoping that Diana might be able to provide them with some other option.

Diana felt moved by Mary's plea and decided to help her. But what could she possibly do? She racked her brain. Who did she know who might be able to help her? Then she suddenly remembered interviewing a doctor several months before about certain new medical procedures. Perhaps he knew of someone.

"I can help this man!" exclaimed the doctor, after she told him the story of Mary's husband. "I myself am a specialist in this area! Mr. L—— may not need his leg to be amputated after all. There are some new up-to-date ways of treating this kind of tumor other than amputation. Send him to me!"

Carl did indeed go through surgery—but not to remove his leg, only the tumor. It was followed by therapy and the complete disappearance of his cancer. Diana's referral had helped save Carl's leg, if not his life.

Mary was overjoyed. She wrote Diana a heartfelt card expressing her thanks. It was so beautifully written and stirring that Diana put it in a memento box in which she saved special items that held great personal meaning. The memento box was stored at the television station where she worked. Similar letters and myriad other mementos piled up in her box, but in her hectic field, she didn't have the time to look at it again.

Almost six years later, Diana was in her late father's home going through a box that contained many of his documents and other possessions when she came across Mary and Carl's letter—now yellowing and frayed—in which the couple had expressed their gratitude for her intervention and help.

"That's strange!" she whispered. "How on earth did this card ever get to be *here*, of all places . . . among Dad's things? I know I put it away at the station, and I never removed it. So what's it doing here, for heaven's sake?"

Because the situation was so odd, Diana felt compelled to reread the note. It was then that alarm bells went off in her head. For weeks, she had noticed—and then dismissed—a strange swelling on her left thigh.

She had assumed she had pulled a muscle while running, and had waited for it to heal by itself. But the swelling had never receded. Diana kept telling herself that she should probably go to a doctor but because of her busy schedule had kept putting it off.

But now, as she reread Mary's note of thanks, Diana's heart began to beat fast. *It wasn't possible, was it?* She seemed to be experiencing the exact same set of symptoms as Carl L——!

The probability that it was the same type of tumor was extremely unlikely—liposarcoma on the thigh is an extremely rare form of cancer—but still, the note provided the impetus she needed. And Diana knew exactly the name of the physician she would see—the same specialist to whom she had referred Carl.

"You're extremely lucky," the doctors she ultimately saw all concurred. "This type of tumor is relatively rare and often goes undetected until it is very large." They reassured her that finding it so early greatly increased her prospects for a complete recovery.

The next months were a whirlwind as Diana underwent several weeks of radiation treatment to shrink the tumor and then, finally, surgery to remove it. Those events were followed by more months of physiotherapy and follow-up testing before things began to return to normal in her life.

Naturally, Diana remembered with immense gratitude the key role that Mary's letter had played in alerting her to her condition and leading her to seek medical help as early as she had. Diana wanted to write Mary to tell her what a difference her note had made in her own life. She went to retrieve the letter so she could get Mary's return address. But she couldn't find it. No matter where she looked, the letter had disappeared again!

~ Bill Cunningham

POEMS FROM MY FATHER

I was never my mother's daughter; it was my father's imprint that I bore instead. Our faces, people exclaimed, were almost identical: our eyes the same unusual hazel color; our "broad-shouldered" physiques (my one true regret) were hewn from similar stone. But beyond physical appearance, our spirits seemed uncommonly linked; there was such an intense connection between us that sometimes I thought we had to be twin souls.

When my father died, I was thirty-three, married, and a mother, but the impact of his death was apocalyptic, despite the three bulwarks of maturity, marital status, and motherhood.

"So how old was he?" insensitive people would ask, as if the age of one's deceased parent matters (the intimation being that it's OK to grieve if he was cut down in his prime, but if he was elderly, authorization to mourn extensively is hereby denied).

As it happened, he was only sixty-two and, yes, far too young to leave this world.

One of the wisest and most comforting customs in the Jewish tradition is the shiva: the seven days of official mourning during which the bereaved are given a context, parameters, and—most important—permission to grieve. During this time, the family is sequestered in the house, and well-wishers visit to extend their sympathy and offer consolation.

On the third day of the shiva, there was a lull between visitors, and I retreated to the kitchen for some quiet contemplation. It was then that I first noticed the stack of papers, written in my father's familiar and beloved spidery handwriting, on the kitchen table. I began to sift through the pile, fingers trembling. Only a few days before, I wouldn't have given the stack a second thought, but now the papers had become transformed into precious relics. There were his signature doodles, scrawled in the margins of the notepaper, the coffee stains that discolored its edges. Only a few short days ago, my father had been vitally alive. Now he was gone, and, ironically, what remained behind to testify to his existence were inanimate objects and lifeless paraphernalia.

I sifted through the papers, searching for clues to his last days. What exactly was I hoping to find? Perhaps, like every other bereaved child (no matter the age), I sought some sign that my father's life force hadn't been wiped out completely. Most of the papers were inconsequential, but then I pulled out a page that made my hands freeze and my heart stop.

It was a poem in Yiddish that my father (a prolific Yiddish writer) had apparently written just before his death—a poem that none of us had known about. My blood ran cold as I read the verses that so eloquently mirrored the despair that he had felt at the end of his life. In rough English translation (which doesn't do the Yiddish couplets justice), the poem read:

> The telephone stands mutely
> Desperately wishing to ring
> Hoping that news of the outside world it can bring
> To the one who waits for a friendly voice

But the phone can't ring, it has no choice
No one is dialing its number to say hello
Where are all the people I used to know?
Everyone has forgotten me, the lines don't hum
The phone is forlorn, and rebuked, it stands dumb.

As I read the poem, my heart ached for my father, who had clearly felt very alone during the last days of his life. I only wished he could have known how mistaken he was about his place in society—how all the pews in the funeral parlor had overflowed with the people who loved and admired him; how many letters, phone calls, baskets, and bouquets had poured into the house to convey anguish at his death.

I thought of the irony inherent in my father's last words: now the phone didn't *stop* ringing with messages of love. Suddenly I stood up and walked—as if a spell had been cast over me—toward my brother's bedroom, where I began to write a poem myself. My father's poem had been entitled "The Silent Phone." Mine, in turn, I called "The Busy Telephone: A Response."

Oh, Father, the phone doesn't stop ringing
As people call from everywhere, your praises singing
Telling of your greatness, your talents commending
With sighs from the heart and tears never-ending
A tragedy, a shame, that you never really felt
The love and esteem in which you were held
And I have to ask them: shouldn't these things have been
    said long ago

To the person who needed to hear them and still . . .
  does not know?
This is the irony of humankind: our sin that we wait
To say the things we feel deeply only when it
  is too late.

When I finished writing the poem, I shook myself out of a mental state that some would label a reverie and others would characterize as "flow," but which I myself felt was more akin to a trance. Looking at the notebook, I shook my head in disbelief. I was not incredulous that I had written a poem, nor was I astonished that, of all the times to write, I had incongruously penned one smack in the middle of shiva. What made me tremble in fear was the fact that I, Yitta Halberstam—whom everyone teased about her broken Yiddish; who barely knew how to write an elementary sentence in the language of her forebears—had just written an entire poem in *flawless* literary Yiddish.

My parents had always spoken Yiddish to one another, but when I was a toddler growing up in Pittsburgh, I was confused by the dissonance of the two languages: Yiddish used exclusively at home, English in the rest of the world. When I turned two and a half and still could barely speak a few words in either language, the pediatrician advised my mother to use English exclusively with me to avoid confusion. Within a few short weeks, I was speaking complete sentences in English, and my parents were never able to revert back to speaking Yiddish with me. Yet, here I was now, an adult, staring at the first poem I had ever written in Yiddish, and, stranger still, it was impeccable.

I was mystified and frightened. How had this happened? When I showed the poem to my mother and siblings later that evening, they looked at me suspiciously. They knew I wasn't capable of this kind of work in Yiddish. Yet they'd all seen me retreat to my brother's bedroom alone and emerge with the poem. Clearly, no one had helped me—so where had the poem come from?

Two days later, I was once again ensconced in the kitchen during an interlude between visitors, and once again I felt called by the muse who seemed to inhabit this room. This was where my father had always worked himself, so that it now became, in the aftermath of his death, elevated to the status of a shrine. Glancing at his work area, I noticed that my father's lamp—an old-fashioned standing lamp—had been pushed into a corner, and I imagined that it looked mournful. *What happens to a man's possessions once he's gone?* I wondered. Do they too somehow feel the pain of his absence?

My mental state of two days before returned. I was transported once again to a different universe. Trancelike, I rose again; once more I took paper and pen into my brother's bedroom and wrote a second poem—this one a paean to "The Standing Lamp." I wrote:

> The standing lamp that my father used is sitting
> shiva alone
> No one pays attention to his keening; no one hears
> him groan

He doesn't understand where his friend has gone;
    the man with whom he was so bound
The man with the words of fire: where can he now
    be found?
It was the lamp's brilliant light that helped the man create
That was his mission in life, after all, to illuminate
The partnership, however, has suddenly been broken
And of the two of them only the lamp is left,
    a lifeless token
His purpose in life is over to which he was born
And now he's pushed into a corner, forgotten and forlorn
No one sees him, no one needs him, he is offended
Against his will, his life's mission has been ended
The lamp is extinguished, gone is its light
The light of my father is extinguished
And now we are plunged into night.

When I finished this second poem, I gazed at it in even greater astonishment than I had felt when I had written the first. For once again, it was written in a highly literary Yiddish—a Yiddish I didn't know, a Yiddish I didn't own. But if I hadn't written it, who had?

A week later, the *Algemeiner Journal*, a Yiddish weekly for which my father had worked as both editor and columnist, published my two poems. Those people who were not my personal friends and did not know my linguistic history congratulated me effusively and praised the work. But those who knew me well and had heard me labor over the same language that was now flawlessly printed in the paper, accosted me skeptically on the streets of Brooklyn.

The confrontation would run along these lines:

"OK, Yitta, I've heard you speak Yiddish. And I know you never wrote a single poem in Yiddish before. So tell me the truth . . . who wrote those poems?"

Having pondered the same question myself, I answered with what I knew was the only possible truth: "My father."

According to the Kabbalah, during the seven days of shiva, the soul of the deceased hovers around the household, to watch family members in a last great burst of yearning and to try to ensure their welfare. The spirit is not yet in transition and, in mysterious ways we cannot discern, is fully present with the family as they grieve.

At the end of the shiva period, it is customary among many Orthodox Jews to leave the house and walk around the block, escorting the departed soul out of the family home forever.

I never wrote a Yiddish poem *before* my father's death, and I never wrote one after. Having considered all the possibilities that could rationally explain how I used words I barely knew and could hardly even recognize, I could come up with only one scenario: the poems had been authored by my father himself; they were his last great creative effort and his own inimitable way of bidding me farewell.

~ *Yitta Halberstam*

ACKNOWLEDGMENTS

Yitta and Judith want to thank . . .
Our phenomenal agent, Carol Mann, and our editor extraordinaire, Barbara Berger, at Sterling Publishing, for bringing this project to fruition with savvy, patience, grace, and a great deal of smarts. Also at Sterling, we thank Yeon Kim for the beautiful interior design, David Ter-Avanesyan for the gorgeous cover, and Josh Redlich in publicity for his amazing professionalism and great creative thinking. Thanks also go to packager Gonzalez Defino and meticulous copyeditor Patricia Fogarty.

Yitta would like to thank . . .
Geri Weiss-Corbley, editor and publisher of www.goodnewsnetwork.org, an awesome inspirational website, and Patricia Raskin, producer and talk show host of the uplifting *Paticia Raskin's Positive Living* programs (http://patriciaraskin.com)—two great women who magnanimously opened their hearts to me and posted my calls for submissions on their websites and newsletters. Also John W. Sloat, creator and host of www.BeyondReligion.com, who also most generously opened his website to me and valiantly helped me try to track down stories. All three went beyond the call of duty in their kind efforts to assist me.

Dr. Bernard Beitman, an extremely open-minded psychiatrist who has studied synchronicities and is working to launch a new interdisciplinary field of coincidence studies, helped direct me to various professionals and websites related to this area as well. Dr. Mordechai Paldiel was incredible in his extraordinary efforts to help me track down one particularly hard-to-find individual. John and Patty Gallagher, beloved proprietors of Harrico pharmacy in Brooklyn, tried valiantly to connect me with other sources, as well. Much appreciation too goes to Barbara Sofer, eminent Israeli journalist, who made a special effort to help me find a source.

Rabbi Joseph and Devorah Telushkin, veritable icons who truly walk their talk, for all their encouragement, kindness, and amazing desire to help me always. Ginny Duffy and Bill Cunningham, who do the same, with amazing goodwill and indomitable "can-do" spirits.

Elie Wiesel, my hero and my late father's friend, who has always bestowed me with great kindness.

Lawyer Jonathan Raven, whom I've met only via e-mail; he went to great lengths to help me track down one particular story—a source of incredible help, kindness, and support.

When the first Small Miracles book was published in 1997, a kind letter was sent my way by Charlie Bono, and we have been in touch ever since, and, he too made exceptional efforts to help me with this project.

Liza Wiemer, an extremely talented writer in her own right, is a devoted friend, a wellspring of love and support. Her encouragement, optimism, and advice are boundless.

If any two people epitomize benevolence, it is Steve Eisenberg and Zeldy Lustig. Their most common responses to any questions are "Yes" or "Of course." This is also true for Rabbi Meir Fund, spiritual leader of Congregation Sheves Achim in Brooklyn. May the world be populated with more people like them.

Raizy Steg and Pesi Dinnerstein are the most incredible friends and pillars of support, love, encouragement, and help that anyone could ever ask for. I am blessed to have them in my life. They are spectacular human beings, and they are God's gifts to me. Although my relationship with Azriela Jaffe has been mainly via e-mail, she is a constant source of guidance, support, and love in my life. Many thanks also to Etta Ansel, Nechama Schreibman, Chaya Sora Sokol, Chanie Reicher, Nechama Rubin, Miriam Maney, and Bella Friedman for being in my life. A great plus of working on the Small Miracles series has been my developing friendship with Judith Leventhal, a zany Lucy to my more sedate Ethel. Our husbands are still scratching their heads, but somehow it works.

My wonderful colleagues at *AMI* magazine, for their constant kindnesses and their tolerance and understanding of my absences during the writing of this book. Special shout-outs to Chaya Laya Moskowitz, Malky Weinberger, and Esty Cinner for always being so helpful in myriad ways. Basha Majerczyk may be one of the most brilliant women I know, and it is an enormous pleasure and privilege to work with her and have her make my prose sing. Rechy Frankfurter, senior editor of *AMI* magazine, constantly leaves me with my mouth agape. How does she know *everything*?

My sister, Miriam Halberstam, a brilliant writer who makes me humble, has been one of my biggest cheerleaders. She constantly encourages me and takes pride in the success of Small Miracles as if it were her own. (She also deviously rearranges books in various bookstores to make sure that Small Miracles titles always end up on the front table!)

My brother, Moishe Halberstam, and his wife, Evelyn, for their love and encouragement, and their children, Chaya and Eli, for giving me such pure, unbridled joy.

My mother-in-law, Sima Mandelbaum, for her devoted, ongoing support, as well as my brothers-in-law and sisters-in-law Chaim and Baila Mandelbaum, and Chaya and Yeruchem Winkler. My most amazing and wonderful children, Yossi and Hena Mandelbaum and Eli and Channa Mandelbaum. Yossi, who is technologically savvy, has tried to "plug" previous Small Miracles books in a host of creative and unusual ways, and has even been kicked off a few websites for mentioning Small Miracles once too often. When Eli was a mere child, on his own (I had absolutely no idea he was doing this) he posted a review of Small Miracles online, saying his name was Dr. Freud Popo. (*Popo*, really?) His quaint choice of pseudonym should have instantly foreshadowed his eventual choice of career— psychology. And no one could ask for nicer daughters-in-law who are helpful and loving in so many ways.

My father, Rabbi Laizer Halberstam, who invested so much in me and taught me everything I know, and my mother, Claire Halberstam, who loved me more than I ever knew.

My rabbi and inspiration, Shlomo Carlebach, who always brought Heaven down to earth, love to people, and people to life, and served as the compelling impetus for my first book, *Holy Brother.*

Finally, *acharon acharon haviv* (the last place is reserved for the most beloved), my dear husband, Motty, who has always thrown his full support behind my endeavors, even when they were off the beaten track and may have raised a few eyebrows. His brilliance, uniqueness, extraordinary kindness, and love of all humanity have permeated my life with great richness. He is my ultimate teacher and the wings on which I fly.

Judith would like to . . .

. . . give a special thanks to Yitta Halberstam. Many times, partnerships begin on solid ground, and then, somewhere along the way, issues arise and the ground gives way. In the case of our partnership, the more I know Yitta, the more I have the privilege of watching her work, the more I see how she gives selflessly to those in need, the more I am in awe of her. We have written a best-selling book, but that blessing pales in comparison to the blessing of having Yitta in my life.

I would like to thank Pesi Dinnerstein, who has been my guiding light. Just like a lighthouse that does not sway regardless of the waves that brush up against it, so too Pesi. No matter what the tides may bring, her valiant support is something that I have come to rely upon.

Ashira Edelman is someone who is always striving to grow. Her insights and wisdom continue to help nurture me, and she is an inspiration to all who are lucky enough to know her and work with her.

Aviva Feldman has a unique way of seeing things and it is her steadfast commitment to leading a life of honesty and simplicity that has made her a great sounding board for ideas that are reflected in this book. For this and so much more, I thank her.

Civia Cahan has a humor and an intelligence that adds so much to my life. I thank her for her unrelenting and unconditional support. It is a true gift to have a friendship that spans decades.

I want to thank Leah Gubitz. Sometimes people come into your life and help crack open a window. Sometimes people can help open a door that was jammed. Through sharing her expansive life experiences with me, Leah peeled away the clouds, which allowed me a peek into the Beyond.

Tova Max has the wisdom of an ageless person though she is so young in years. She is constantly pointing the way toward an even more enlightened path. Sometimes I lead and she follows, and sometimes it is the other way around. Either way, it is a journey that has been a treasure.

I want to thank my mother, who has always expected the world of me and demanded that I expect that of myself. Regardless of any achievement I have made, my mother has always clapped for me and then pointed even higher. The sky is not the limit when it comes to her appreciation, admiration, and support for her children. I am blessed to have a mother who has poured so much love into me so that I can take that pitcher and pour that love into my children.

I want to thank my two sisters. My sister Hedy Feiler and her husband, Myer, who together have raised children whom I am proud to call my family: Jack and Huvie, Aviva and Tzvi, Yisroel and Rachelli, David and Mimi, Anschel and Ettala and Hershy. Their children, their effervescent personalities, their songs and dances brighten every family gathering and bring joy to all. My sister Esty and her husband, Jordan, bring so much humor and love into our lives. Regardless of the circumstances, Esty will find a way to make everyone laugh right through it all. A special shout-out to her son, Aron Tzvi, whom we all adore.

And lastly, I want to thank my husband and children: Jules, who has always been my greatest support—I owe him a gratitude that cannot be put into words. And our three daughters who are our three shining stars; Arielle, Shira, and Tehilla. You are all my inspiration. You are my blessing. You are my Beyond.

One last word from Yitta and Judith:
One last thank-you . . . to God. There are many far worthier writers and books out there in the universe who deserve to capture the imagination of the American people. Tens of thousands of new books are cranked out each year, and sometimes, sadly, the best fall through the cracks. We know that the Small Miracles series could just as easily have shared their fate, and that it is only because of your special blessing, God, that it has over two million copies in print. We are deeply cognizant of that fact—and enormously grateful—always.

CONTRIBUTORS

Winnie Alley has always wanted to write. She loves to travel and has a keen interest in spirituality and metaphysics. She lives in Bedford, Nova Scotia. Her story "Going Up" was published in *Elevator World* magazine.

Cheryl Anderton, a retired registered nurse, is a mother and grandmother. She is also a musician and a student of genealogy. Her husband is a retired airline captain. After his career of thirty-five years, the couple moved back to his birthplace, Winchester, Tennessee, the town in which her story in this book unfolded.

Bernard Beitman, MD, is the first psychiatrist to research synchronicity since Carl Jung. He is a silent father of the emerging discipline called Coincidence Studies. A graduate of Yale and Stanford and former chair of the Department of Psychiatry at the University of Missouri-Columbia, he has received two national awards for his psychotherapy training program. (For more, see www.drbeitman.com.)

Cindy Lubar Bishop was born and raised in White Plains, New York. She worked for some years in theater with director Robert Wilson, produced performance pieces of her own, worked as an administrative assistant, and has made three short documentary films. Cindy lives with her husband, Neil, in Santa Rosa, California, and has a practice that combines synchronicity and dreamwork.

Rea Bochner is a professional writer and editor, and a columnist for *Ami* magazine. When not crafting copy, Rea is a full-time mother, washerwoman, chef, chauffeur, housekeeper, and referee. She lives in New Jersey with her husband, their three sons, and eight piles of clean laundry waiting to be folded.

Jamie Cat Callan is the author of the internationally best-selling books *French Women Don't Sleep Alone, Bonjour Happiness!* and *Ooh La La!: French Women's Secrets to Feeling Beautiful Every Day*. She is also the creator of *The Writer's Toolbox: Creative Games and Exercises for Inspiring the "Write" Side of Your Brain* and has had a lifelong love of boots.

Lindsey Cresswell is a bank clerk who lives with her husband, Colin, and two sons, Scott and Jack, in Durham, England.

Bill Cunningham is a writer who lives in Miami whose overlapping interests are spirituality and poetry. He finds the great joy of his life in the gift of his family and beloved friends.

Wayne W. Dyer, PhD, is an internationally renowned best-selling author and speaker in the field of self-development. He is the author of over thirty books, has created many audio programs and videos, and has appeared on thousands of television and radio shows, including many PBS specials.

Alina S. Fenton was born in Cuba, where she remembers a happy, carefree childhood. All that changed when Fidel Castro took power in 1960. When she was ten years old, her family left the island and started a new life in Miami. In 1969 Alina married her high school sweetheart, Jimmy Fenton. Jimmy worked with the Exxon Company for thirty years, and the family moved around quite a bit. Alina was a stay-at-home mom, making room for tennis, gardening, and arts and crafts, and she was always busy with her children. In 1989 a close friend suggested they travel to Mexico to buy Mexican pewter items to sell to friends, and Fabulous Mexicrafts became a successful business that lasted for sixteen years! In 1994 Alina and her husband suffered an unimaginable and devastating loss when their twenty-two-year-old son, Jimmy, became the victim of a homicide in their own community of Coconut Grove.

Their daughter, Alison, is now married to a wonderful, loving man and is a mother to three healthy, beautiful boys. This November Alina and her husband will celebrate their forty-fifth wedding anniversary.

B. Lynn Goodwin is the owner of Writer Advice (www.writeradvice.com) and the author of *You Want Me to Do What? Journaling for Caregivers*. She has published numerous short stories and essays in regional and national publications and online, including the *Oakland Tribune*, the *Contra Costa Times*, *Hip Mama*, and the *Sun*. A former teacher, she conducts workshops and writes reviews for Story Circle Network (www.storycircle.org).

Lois Greene Stone, writer and poet, has been syndicated worldwide. Her poetry and personal essays are included in both hardcover and softcover anthologies. Collections of her personal items, photos, and memorabilia are in major museums, including twelve divisions of the Smithsonian.

Cena Gross-Abergel was born and raised in Los Angeles, the youngest of three children. Her parents were first-generation Americans with roots in Poland and Hungary. She has been married for thirty-eight years, and is both a mother and a grandmother. She is thrilled that she has been able to pay tribute to her eighty-four-year-old mother, Sarah, the subject of her story in this book, who lives in Culver City, California.

Faigie Heiman, an accomplished short-story writer and essayist, was born and raised in Brooklyn, New York, and has lived in Jerusalem, Israel, since 1960. She is the author of a popular memoir entitled *Girl for Sale*, published in honor of her mother's one-hundredth birthday.

David Kukoff is a screenwriter, professor, and author. His first novel, *Children of the Canyon*, about a boy growing up in the Los Angeles counterculture of the 1970s, was published in March 2013 and was re-released in a special edition in February 2014.

Cheryl Kupfer is the daughter of two Holocaust survivors from Poland, whose parents and many siblings, nieces, and nephews were murdered by the Nazis. She says the first thing her eyes likely focused on while in her mother's arms were the blue numbers tattooed on her forearm. Her concepts of grandparents were *yahrzeit* (memorial) candles and the wraiths she believed flew around in the synagogue sanctuary, where as a child she was rushed out before the adults recited Yiskor, the soulful prayer said in remembrance of dead relatives.

Karen M. Jordan is a retired speech and language teacher who was born and raised in New York City. She is the proud mother of two children, Michael and Debra. Karen loved to write from an early age, but this is her first story to be published.

Dot Lenhart is a longtime professional gardener and amateur bird-watcher who lives in Vermont.

Robin Davina Meyerson was an award-winning marketing communications director for a Fortune 200 company and an adjunct business professor before she followed her heart to focus on family and community. She grew up in Australia, Malaysia, and Europe, experiencing the world's cultures. Robin fueled her Jewish soul by writing her first book, *A Son Returns*. Robin was the cofounder and publisher of *Jewish Spirit* magazine and served on the board of the Jewish Tuition Organization, raising millions for Jewish day-school scholarships. She volunteers with the Jewish Burial Society (Chevrah Kadisha), where she helps prepare bodies for burial. She helped create www.jewishdeathandmourning.org and www.peacefulreturn.org. She's mommy to five beautiful children and has been proudly married for twenty-three years. She can be reached at rdmtraveldiscovery@cox.net.

Penina Neiman is a freelance writer of nonfiction. She specializes in inspirational writing and has published dozens of times in a variety of Jewish publications. She has recently coauthored a highly successful book called *The Mountain Family: An Appalachian Family of 12—and Their Fascinating Journey to Judaism*, published by Shaar Press.

Joan Otto married Howard Otto, the love of her life, in 1954. They stayed married for fifty-eight years until Howard's death. They have five children, thirteen grandchildren, and six great-grandchildren. That's everything anyone could ask for.

Erin Pavlina is a spiritual teacher, intuitive counselor, and author. She has written more than seven hundred articles on her blog at www.erinpavlina.com, which is read by more than one million people worldwide.

Gail Raab has a BS in journalism from the University of Memphis. She wrote and produced radio commercials for WSB in Memphis, and wrote a newspaper column called "Gab with Gail Raab" for the *Birmingham Jewish Star*. She has read hundreds (maybe thousands) of books on the Afterlife and has experienced numerous miracles from beyond in her own life.

Jonathan Raven is an experienced attorney and business counselor, and a self-described empiricist, whose undergraduate emphasis on behavioral sciences none-theless left him with an open eye toward unseen things that make the human experience and individual people unique, remarkable, and simultaneously predict-able and inexplicable.

Anna Rawlings experienced the loss of her brother and that led her on a long and sometimes challenging journey. She struggled to accept his sudden death as she worked to redefine her life, at the same time as she was beginning her teaching career. Writing and journaling have been an important part of her healing pro-cess, the source of her stories in this book. Anna is a teacher, workshop leader, and holistic pulsing practitioner who is currently developing a well-being prac-tice in order to share what her experiences have taught her. Anna's interests lie in working with sensitive children and those experiencing stress and anxiety, as well as in supporting their families. Anna lives in Sydney, Australia, with her hus-band, two young children, and chocolate Labrador, Charlie. Her website is www.annarawlings.com.

Liliane Aura Ritchie has touched thousands of people's lives, with a high quality of wisdom and kindness, though her writings, teachings, paintings, and coaching. She has published *Masters and Miracles: Divine Interventions*, as well as *A Gift of Love: Holding On to Your Highest Dreams* and *Answers from Above: Connecting with God*; these books can be found on http://www.refuah.net/gallery.php as well as on Amazon.com. She and her husband, Dr. Joshua Ritchie, MD, now live in Jerusalem. They are blessed with five wonderful children.

Shaul and Brany Rosen are the founders and directors of A TIME, an internation-ally acclaimed organization that offers advocacy, education, guidance, research, and support to Jewish couples struggling with reproductive health and infertility. For more information, please consult www.atime.org.

Hindy Rosenberg was the primary caretaker for twenty years of her mother, Miriam Perlstein, the protagonist of her Auschwitz story in this book, when she was stricken with a debilitating stroke. Hindy strongly believes that everything she is today she learned from her mother, an indomitable, unforgettable, and beloved woman who died this past year.

Laya Saul is known for her award-winning self-help book for young adults *You Don't Have to Learn Everything the Hard Way—What I Wish Someone Had Told Me.* You can find encouragement and inspiration from Laya at her websites: www. AuntLaya.com and www.NurturingWomen.com.

Bina Simon is a wife, mom, and registered nurse in Chicago.

Janet White Sperber enjoys life with her husband and their dog, Joey, in San Juan Capistrano, California.

Chaya Sarah Stark is a singer, dancer, actress, writer, and educator who lives in Brooklyn with her family. This story was written in loving memory of her father, Ephraim ben Yitzchok Isaac Schwartz.

Leslie Weistreich is a businessman living in New York City. He has three children (a son and two daughters). He devotes much of his free time, energy, and resources to organizations in the United States and Israel that benefit the Jewish community.

Liza Wiemer is the author of two adult nonfiction books, *Extraordinary Guidance: How to Connect with Your Spiritual Guides*, published by Random House, and *Waiting for Peace: How Israelis Live with Terrorism*, from Gefen Publishing. Her young adult novel *Hello?* will be published by Spencer Hill Contemporary in 2015. Her websites include www.WhoRuBlog.com; you can also find her on www. goodreaders.com/author/show/433276.LizaWiemer and Twitter@LizaWiemer.

Daniel S. Wise is an American playwright, director, producer, and author. His productions have been presented in New York—on Broadway and off-Broadway—as well as in Japan, Russia, China, South Korea, Taiwan, Singapore, Britain, and South Africa. He is an ordained rabbi.

CREDITS

"The Candlelight Inn," pages 78–83
1 Dyer, Wayne, interview by Bonnie Hunt, the *Bonnie Hunt Show,* syndication, 2009.
  Referenced throughout.
2 Ibid.
3 Wayne Dyer, *I Can See Clearly Now,* 2014, Hay House, Inc., Carlsbad, CA, p. 144.
4 Ibid, pp. 145–46.

Excerpts from *I Can See Clearly Now* and the *Bonnie Hunt Show* reproduced with
  kind permission from Wayne Dyer.

"The Will," pages 134–41
Sources include:
Mary Roach, *Spook: Science Tackles the Afterlife* (New York: W. W. Norton, 2005),
  pp. 241–62.
Daniel Barefoot, *Piedmont Phantoms: North Carolina's Haunted Hundred,* vol. 2
  (Winston-Salem, NC: John F. Blair, 2002), pp. 32–36.
John Harden, *Tar Heel Ghosts* (Chapel Hill, NC: University of North Carolina Press, 1954).
Miles Edward Allen, "Where There's a Will," 2012, Survival Top 40–Case #73–ESS = 255c
  ÆCES (Association for Evaluation and Communication of Evidence for Survival)
  http://www.aeces.info/Top40/Cases_51-75/Case73_WhereWill.pdf

"The Shofar," pages 181–95
Sources include:
Sheryl Silver Ochayon, "The Shofar from Skarzysko-Kamienna," the International School
  for Holocaust Studies, Yad Vashem, http://www.yadvashem.org/yv/en/education/
  artifacts/shofar.asp and http://www.yadvashem.org/yv/en/exhibitions/live_with_honor/
  shofar.asp
Barbara Sofer, "The Story of a Shofar," *Jerusalem Post,* September 28, 2006,
  http://www.jpost.com/Opinion/Columnists/Story-of-a-shofar

**Excerpted from other books in the Small Miracles series by Yitta Halberstam and
Judith Leventhal:**
Janet White Sperber, "The Birthday Call," pages 225–27, originally published in
  Small Miracles for Families: Extraordinary Coincidences That Reaffirm Our Deepest Ties
  (Holbrook, MA: Adams Media, 2003).

Bill Cunningham, "The Memento Box," pages 237–39; and Yitta Halberstam, courtesy of
  Sherman Ladin, "Medical School Miracle," pages 228–31, both originally published in
  Small Miracles of Love & Friendship: Remarkable Coincidences of Warmth and Devotion
  (Holbrook, MA: Adams Media, 2002).

Yitta Halberstam, "Poems from My Father," pages 240–46; and Gail Raab, "The Biggest
  Rose," pages 232–33, both originally published in *Small Miracles For The Jewish Heart:
  Extraordinary Coincidences from Yesterday and Today* (Holbrook, MA: Adams Media,
  2002).

Alina S. Fenton, "Jimmy," pages 220–24, originally published in *Small Miracles for Women:
  Extraordinary Coincidences of Heart and Spirit* (Holbrook, MA: Adams Media, 2000).